LIVING WITH JESUS

AND THE BOOK OF JOB

DURING LENT

by Elaine M. Ward

To Anabel,

who shares with me

wonder

To Chuck

who teaches me

wisdom

In the gift of their friendship.

LIVING WITH JESUS AND THE BOOK OF JOB DURING LENT

by Elaine M. Ward

Copyright ©1995

Educational Ministries, Inc.

ISBN 1-877871-94-X

Educational Ministries, Inc.
165 Plaza Drive
Prescott, AZ 86303
800-221-0910

TABLE OF CONTENTS

INTRODUCTION

Living With Jesus and the Book of Job During Lent is six sessions based on Job's (and our) questions concerning the meaning of existence, such as: Is this all? What are friends for? Why emptiness and misery? Where shall wisdom be found? What is resurrection? Where is my Redeemer?

The book of Job is part of the wisdom tradition. An overview of wisdom literature is found in the introduction. It can be used as a study session, bringing the unit "Living With Jesus and the Book of Job During Lent" to seven sessions that include Ash Wednesday, Palm Sunday, and Easter, if desired.

This study can be used as individual or group study during Lent, for personal spiritual devotions, or as a series of sermons, reflecting the questions of Job and the Passion of Jesus.

I recently became acquainted with Job. Oh, I had heard of him by hearsay, you know, "patient as Job." I had given him brief nods of recognition in passing, but I had never sat with him on the ashheap, in the garbage of life, listening to his cries for days at a time. When at last I did, the poetry seemed to say, "This is a text for today!"

The book of Job asks questions all of us ask: Why is there evil and injustice? Why do we suffer? Does God care? What are friends for? Where is my redeemer? Where shall wisdom be found?

As I was growing up, I was taught the theology of the prophets and the priests. The prophets asked (and answered) "Is there a word from the Lord?" The priestly tradition taught that good comes to the righteous and the evil suffer. Somewhere I missed the strain that would allow me to make room for diversity, ambiguity, paradox, and trust based on love, which for me is the nature of God. Yet the book of Job was there all along. This meditation book is an attempt to introduce a beginning study of the wisdom tradition.

5

"The Book of Job is a masterwork of the human spirit—or many believe, of God's Spirit...But Job is also one of the most perplexing books ever written...When friends asked, 'Why are you studying Job?', I wanted to reply, 'Why isn't everyone else? How can they resist it?' "[1]

When the poets of the book of Job wanted to defend their theology, which was in opposition to "God rewards the just and punishes the evil," they borrowed an ancient folktale and set their poetry (and theology) within it.

Job's experience did not fit his theology, as a friend once said to me, "My experience is changing so fast, my theology has to run to keep up with it." I have learned through traumatic and joyous experiences that "my" way is not the only way, at times not even the best way, that it is possible that God has something better in store for us than that for which we pray.

Because I believe in the power of stories to describe experience rather than to define for knowledge's sake, I have woven parables into the prose. Stories elicit wonder, an appreciative affirmation of the heart and spirit when the head does not understand. The power of the story is shown in the example of placing Jesus on the cross as a criminal, one who was trying to rob the religious authorities of their story which gave life and meaning to some of the people, the privileged and the ones who had the "right" faith. The rest were left out. It was "status quo" all the way.

Stories present possible answers to questions, nurture the soul, ignite the imagination, and give delight, presenting images that invite the reader/hearer to find meaning and care for the soul.

Sacred stories symbolize our spiritual understanding. It is the joyous task of the preacher, teacher, all Christians to seek to invite persons into the parables. Job is such a parable for today.

Wisdom prefers song and dance and imagination to "right answers." Job asked many of the questions we ask today, so we study Job with our heads, but we also experience a poignant participation in Job's suffering that helps us learn with our hearts. It is a story in which we can reside.

The book of Job provides me a place to live. I feel as if I have found a home. The roof leaks, there are cracks in the door, the windows are smeared, but it's a home. Or to change the metaphor, discovering wisdom literature is for me discovering a hidden spring of fresh water that revives my weary, questioning spirit. I wonder why it has been a secret for so

6

long—at least from me.

Included are questions for discussion and activities in which to participate, with background material for understanding and celebrating the biblical wisdom tradition.

INTRODUCTION TO WISDOM EDUCATION

WISDOM EDUCATION IS:

1. _Experiential._ I know because I have experienced and reflected, and human experience can be trusted. Wisdom affirms engaging in tradition but balancing that with honoring one's own experience, learning to listen to and trust one's own experiences.

The book of Job is a story that takes place anywhere, anytime. God and Satan debate Job's motivation for fearing God. "Does Job fear God for nothing?" asked Satan. Is there such a thing as disinterested piety? God gives Job into the power of Satan, who takes from him his possessions, servants, his sons and daughters, and his reputation. Yet Job is innocent and out of his suffering, pain, and innocence asks, "Why do bad things happen to good people?" What kind of God can allow the torture of the innocent? These are the questions asked during and after the Holocaust. They are the questions we ask out of our own experiences with suffering.

Whereas Job speaks from his experience and emotions, his aches and sores, his friends' responses are cool and calculated, coming from their heads. They are the premeditated answers of their traditions of faith.

Reading and reflecting on Job, church educators ask, "Is my teaching, my commitment, full of premeditated answers or my passionate longing for God? Do I feel the questions with which my students are struggling? Do I listen and empathize or answer before asked? Do I ask questions or give answers? Do I help my students to ask, "What if...?" Am I willing to take the time required for prayer and planning, for relating the materials of the session (my sermon) with my and their experiences?

We learn from our experiences and our reflection on those experiences. One of the early church fathers said that the glory of God is a person fully alive. And one of the Hasidic Masters taught, "A human being who has not a single hour for his own every day is not a human being."

Placing human experience and reason above cultic tradition (the actions of God in history), King Solomon (1 Kings 3:9) asked the Lord for a "listening heart." Wisdom literature suggests discerning the circumstances, the right place at the right time for the right person. It is concerned with the everydayness of life. What do I need to know for the living of life?

Job gained his wisdom through his experience of pain and suffering.

> A Kashmiri tale, "How Great is Your Wisdom!" tells of a discontented man, sitting under a nut tree, thinking how hard life was, when he observed a large pumpkin vine near by, and on the vine a large pumpkin was growing.
>
> "If God had been more clever, we would have no misery in the world," the man groaned aloud. "Just see how foolish God was when He created. Here is a large strong tree with hundreds of small nuts growing on it and there on that weak vine grows an immense pumpkin. How could God make such a mistake? It should have been just the other way around, the large pumpkin on the mighty tree and the small nuts on the weak vine. Who says God is wise?"
>
> The man continued to moan, groan and complain, when suddenly one of the nuts fell from the tree, landing on his head. Startled, the man looked up. Then he jumped up quickly and fell on his knees, praying. "Forgive me, God, I know not of what I speak. If one of those pumpkins had fallen on my head from the tree, I would now be dead! How great is your wisdom, O Lord! How great is your wisdom!"

2. Playful. In a class on Job,[2] after talking about the "playfulness" of wisdom, we created titles for three chapters of Job (29-31). Having divided into three groups, we spent twenty minutes playfully creating titles, which were then written on the board for all groups to read. Having read all the titles, the professor asked, "Did they get the titles right?"

There was silence. For the first time in the seven consecutive days of living together with Job, no one spoke.

The professor wrinkled his brow in confusion and asked again, "Did they get the titles right?"

The class burst into laughter, again beginning to play.

You see, the "right answer" is inappropriate to wisdom literatrue. The question "teases" us into thinking. "Creation had its root in wonder, its fulfillment in joy."[3]

8

"What are you doing?"

Wisdom answers, "I am!"

Play provides liberating forms for the enjoyment of God and of life, of just being, breaking the bonds that alienate us from one another and from real life. It is the celebration of "I am!" rather than what I am doing. The calm enjoyment of existence extols the least, the lost, and the little.

Creation is God's play, the place that displays God's glory:

Read this story:

> After God had created the earth and the heavens, all the animals and birds and Adam and Eve, God retired from the hard work of creation. During the week after creation, God went to visit Adam and Eve, who lived in a little grass shack under the great apple tree.
>
> "Well, children," God said, "how are things going? Is everything O.K.?"
>
> "Oh yes, indeed," replied Adam. "Everything is fine. Eve and I love all that you have made."
>
> "Yes," added Eve, "it is good; however...it's kind of stuffy here in the garden."
>
> "I hadn't noticed," replied God. "Well, dear, nothing is perfect in this life. Enjoy yourselves!"
>
> Two days later, God came to visit again, greeting them as usual: "Well, children, how are things going?"
>
> "It's O.K., God, but there's nothing to do in the evening after we've worked in the garden all day," said Adam.
>
> "Hmmm..," said God. "I never thought of that as a problem. Perhaps you could dance?"
>
> "Dance?" said both Adam and Eve together. "It's so animal!"
>
> "Well..," said God, "it was just an idea. But..." God looked down at the ground.
>
> "What is it? You have something on your mind."
>
> "Well, I have been visited by a delegation of dinosaurs. They are uspset because the two of your are living together but aren't married."
>
> "What is that?" asked Eve.

9

"It is a ritual of becoming one for life."

"Who needs marriage, God?" asked Adam. "Why do you listen to those uptight dinosaurs? Their ideas are so old and outdated!"

"I know I've warned them about their conservative attitudes, but you know how much weight they throw around in the garden. I have resisted coming out of retirement, but it looks as if we won't have any peace in the garden until I create marriage."

God went to the drawing board and designed a beautiful ritual that two human beings could celebrate together.

On Saturday, Adam and Eve got married. It was a garden wedding, and all creation attended. Everyone was pleased because everyone was at peace.

Sunday morning, God awoke with a shock. "I didn't give them a wedding present! What can I do? It's Sunday morning and everything is closed!" God began to comb her hair as she thought.

About mid-morning all the creatures in the garden were startled to hear a giant crack of thunder and they all knew what it meant: God had just had an idea. The dinosaurs groaned, thinking of the change it meant.

Adam and Eve were doing nothing, since it was Sunday, when a great package wrapped in silver paper with a wonderful pink-ribboned bow slowly floated out of the sky. Quickly, they undid the wrappings and opened the box. Looking inside they saw NOTHING! "The box is empty!" they said to each other.

At that the pink ribbon on the ground stood up and swayed to and fro slowly in a delightful little dance. The wrapping-paper stood up, whirled around and skipped off down the lawn. Something new was present in the garden, but it was...invisible!

The leaves on their stems began to dance, the tall grasses moved. "It's no longer stuffy in the garden," Eve cried, as invisible fingers played in the hair of the young couple. Eve looked at Adam... "Let's dance—like the ribbon, the leaves and the grasses!"

And so it was that on the second seventh day God created the wind. It was a most special creature, for it was a vital part of God herself. She had let her hair down, and in an act of great sensuality was slowly stroking the body of her creation with her hair! That act of love set seeds airborne, gave coolness to the garden, and sent sailing ships dancing across the tops of waves. Even to this day, each time we feel our hair being "let down by the wind," we too are called to freedom, to the dance and joy of life![4]

3. _A calling into growth:_ The abundant life of Jesus spoke about bringing us, is a new way of sensing and seeing with faith. With faith one "sees" with more than one's eyes. Our faith imagination encourages us to act out and try on truth, awakening us to that which is beyond all knowledge through intuition, imagination, and the unconscious.

"What I am about to say is true, though it may never have happened," begins the storyteller.

The theologian William Lynch calls faith "the superb life of the imagination," and Amos Wilder said that just because we lack imagination is no reason to think that the ancients did. The poet Wallace Stevens called imagination "the power of the mind over the possibility of things."

Faith is dynamic. It changes; grows and decreases. Doubt is not necessarily disbelief. Doubt can be re-visioning. Jacob, Job, and Jeremiah remind us that doubt can be the impetus to deeper trust, for faith is not proof, faith is beyond belief. Faith is trust that brings possibility into being.

Questions call us into growth. The wisdom approach asks provocative questions, listens to all answers, and celebrates learning together, aware that answers depend on the particular situatation to which they are being addressed. Asking creative questions includes:

1. maintaining an open environment where learners feel free to express their own thoughts and feelings,

2. preparing learners for the possibility of questions having more than one right answer,

3. asking open questions that invite opinions and feelings,

4. allowing enough silence and time for thinking and responding,

5. giving everyone an opportunity to participate,

6. asking the question before directing it to one learner,

7. using an informational question as a springboard for creative questions.

Jesus said, "We piped to you and you would not dance." Opening our eyes and ears to the wonders in and about us calls us to new growth.

4. Relationship. Relationship is at the core of the process of learning and living. Wisdom education is community-oriented rather than teacher-oriented. It is power-with and power-among rather than power-over, for there is a sense of connectiveness, nurturing, creativity in wisdom education.

An adequate language to describe another perception of reality, a language of mystery and paradox, requires work on the hearer's part. "Sophia," or wisdom education calls us to honesty, demanding reflection and response from a wide variety of voices. Most of us want to "nail down," to codify, to fix in formulas our beliefs, but "what if" they are living? What if they will not be bound or imprisoned in rote, memorized answers? Experiencing relationship with God is a living relationship.

Discuss "living" faith, faith as a verb.

5. Universal. Wisdom education borrows from other cultures and religions, for all people in all times have been concerned with the questions of life and death, with the challenges of coping with their current circumstances.

6. A seeking for wholeness, the spiritual and physical in unity, celebrating the goodness of God's creation, and making all things new. We die to old perception to arise anew to Christ's way of seeing and being in the world.

Society rewards us for our Western scientific way of seeing, for our rational, reasonable thinking. Yet we are also creatures of feelings, of imagination and creativity, and the secret is integration. Each side must be developed and function for the individual to be able to choose which mode of thinking/feeling is most appropriate at that time and place.

Creative individuals "link" the known to the unknown, the head to the heart, knowledge to experience, and the parts to the whole. One side of the brain differentiates, the other celebrates. One inspects, directs, and selects, while the other waits, mates, and creates.

I like an orderly, dependable world, where the sky stays in its place and land stays in its place and night follows day and day follows night and yet are filled with both harmony and dissonance and diversity to make up the balance rhythm we call life. God, the Source of all life is the unity of the universe, or as Meister Eckhart said, "God is a great underground river that no one can dam up and no one can stop."

Wisdom education is not compartmentalized. It teaches vulnerability, asking questions rather than giving answers, encouraging a gentle boldness, enticing a teasing trust. It believes that faith and works are not separated. Life is a gift. Do our actions show that we are really "truly grateful" for what we are given?

Tell (or read) this story.

Penny Defore stated her reason for spending her nineteenth Christmas in a Korean orphanage: "I had been given so much that I wanted to give something back."[5]

Penny Defore is the daughter of actor Don Defore. In 1960 Penny went to Korea as a starry-eyed teenager to work as a volunteer in an orphanage there. Her desire began when she was thirteen and visited her father on the movie set for a film about Col. Dean Hess of the U.S. Air Force who founded the orphanage. About 25 children from the orphanage were in the film, and when she heard the stories of the handships they had endured, she was appalled. From that moment Penny began to raise money for the children and soon felt that God wanted her to go to Korea.

On Christmas Day, at 19, she was 7,000 miles from home!

Awaking that Christmas Day, in her clothes, to biting cold, no electricity, no running water, no radiators, Penny grabbed her Bible and ran to the dormitories to shiver with the 250 orphans, Christmas singing, and the spirit of love.

On that day she also awoke to a problem worse than physical deprivations, she awoke to the problem of evil. Evil is whatever diminishes life and here life was greatly diminished!

Penny awoke to a world different from her own, a world of harsh punishments for the oprhans, where standards of morality and honesty confused and frightened her, and Penny, in a new and strange country, was alone.

But Penny was not alone. Penny prayed. In the past she had found peace of mind in the presence of God. Now she faced the terrible awareness that perhaps her dream was not God's will, but her own, the romantic desire of a self-centered child.

Penny continued her duties and found pleasure in the children, but she could not please those in authority. They felt her difference and viewed her with suspicion. At last she turned the whole affair over to God—whether to stay or whether to leave.

Three days later she was invited to work in a church clinic for crippled children in another city nearby and live with an American family who had a daughter Penny's age.

As she left she felt confused. On the one hand her prayer had been answered. On the other hand, she left, having failed.

What did Penny learn from her experience? She learned that when one door is closed, God opens another. "You must also be prepared to suffer defeat," Penny wrote.

Penny learned, as the wisdom tradition celebrated, that the wise person learns through their own experience.

Two years later, when Penny wrote of her experience, she was thankful because of that Christmas in Korea, a Christmas that taught her that both success and failure are a part of being alive, and life is a gift of God.

9. <u>A process that uses stories and metaphors.</u> The power of the metaphor is that it helps us to see, while allowing mystery, similarity and dissimilarity, and avoiding fixing words into rotted forms. Metaphors invite hearers/readers to imagine and provoke their under-standing from their own experiences. It is a way of "easing" the learner into thinking. Jesus used metaphors in his parables of the kingdom of God.

Ask yourself, "What is the key metaphor in the story above?" Evoke, give birth to or draw from the hearers' memory, metaphors that enrich. What image is created when you hear, "Don't turn the water into the wine"?

Fred Craddock, a master preacher, is skilled in the use of metaphors:[6] Writing of the language-lag in the church:

"..unfortunately, the church has no retirement program for old words that fought well at Nicea, Chalcedon and Augsburg; they are kept in the line of march even if the whole mission is slowed to a snail's pace and observers on the side are bent double in laughter."[7]

"Rarely, if ever, in the history of the church have so many firm periods slumped into commas and so many triumphant exclamation points curled into question marks."[8]

"Where have all the absolutes gone? The old thunderbolts rust in the attic while the minister tries to lead his people through the morass of relativities and proximate possibilities."[9]

"He wants to speak and yet he needs more time for more certainty before speaking. His is often the misery of one who is always pregnant but never ready to give birth."[10]

The Christian church knows the power of metaphors and symbols, such as "living water, "the bread of life," "Holy Spirit," "reign of God," altar, sacrifice, Messiah, the "Word of God," "tree of life," Jerusalem the Golden, the whole armor of God, "God," etc. St. Paul's angels, archangels, principalities and power. These symbols create not only images but emotions, as well.

When Paul spoke of the church, he spoke of a body: "For just as the body is one and has many members, and all the members of the body, though many, are one body, so it is with Christ. For in the one Spirit we were all baptized into one body—Jews or Greeks, slaves or free—and we were all made to drink of one Spirit. Indeed, the body does not consist of one member but of many. If the foot would say, "Because I am not a hand..." (1 Corinthians 12:12-15).

It is our task in the church to keep alive Christian metaphors and the symbols so that they remain fresh and relevant and participatory to the hearer/seer in the faith community. When the church or any hearer cuts itself off from metaphor or symbol, Christianity becomes empty conformity, obedience without imagination. It is not an easy job to prevent creeds from becoming codified, religious instincts from becoming institutionalized, and sacred stories from becoming conventional morality, written dogma or doctrine, thus removing the authentic, dynamic religious element in them, which is the subjective encounter and dialogue with God.

Stories are extended metaphors, words proceeding from the breath or pen of the storyteller to create meaning. They speak of human experience; life and death, joy and pain, success and failure, the beginning and sometimes the ending of earth, and moon, wind and water. They are rooted in common soil, common experience, fed by the imagination and the nourishing sunshine of hope in order to bloom with wonder and delight.

The Christian teacher or preacher does not speak in abstract terms to define who God is and what God has done, but she or he tells a story, as Peter did in respones to the question, "What does it mean?" (Acts 2:12)

Christianity is a story. It is the story of God putting on human flesh and placing his tent among us.

Trying to make Mystery rational is frustrating, if not impossible. We stutter, we stumble, we shudder before the Majesty and Mystery of God. We try to put our wonder and confusion, our faith and our fear into words, not to define but to describe. So we teach and preach the story. Sometimes it is God's story as told in scripture. Sometimes it is our story of seeking God, or of trying to live a life fully and obedient to God's plan revealed by Jesus, the Christ.

Religious language is a language of wonder and mystery, stories and metaphors. Our perception of the world is built on the stones and stories of our ancestors.

"It is as if the Mythmaker has transformed science, turning science into myth," writes Larry Dossey in Space, Time & Medicine[11], quoting Niels Bohr: "..when it comes to atoms, language can be used only as in poetry. The poet too is not nearly so concerned with describing facts as with creating images and establishing mental connections...Quantum theory...provides us with a striking illustration of the fact that we can fully understand a connection though we can only speak of it in images and parables..."

10. A celebration of creation, seeing wonder in every day. Jesus told his hearers to consider the lilies of the fields and the birds of the air. Jesus' images in his parables were from nature: fig trees and seeds and vineyards, and such.

Tell or read this story:

> *Always when such things as heaven and the hereafter came up for discussion, the same Little Old Lady left the Senior Citizens Central Park Discussion Group and wandered off into a small coppice through which a brook meandered.*
>
> *Perplexed, a Ministerial Counselor followed her one day and, from a discreet distance, saw her bend to a flower, run her hand over the rough bark of a tree, finger the curve of a stone, blow gently on a spider's web.*
>
> *When she wandered off once more and was again returning from among the trees, the Counselor stopped her to ask, "You keep wandering away. Is something wrong?"*
>
> *"Well, yes.." she answered.*
>
> *"Can I help?" the Counselor asked.*
>
> *"You can," she replied briskly.*
>
> *"Tell me how," the Counselor said.*
>
> *"Stop babbling about the hereafter and sing instead of the glories of the hereabouts and the beauties of* this day.*"[12]*

"Everywhere I look I see fire: that which isn't flint is tinder, and the whole world sparks and flames," writes Annie Dillard in Pilgrim at Tinker Creek.[13] There is potential holiness of the uncommon commonplace, if we allow wonder its proper place in our perception of the world.

Some people, especially young children and mystics, encounter all things with wonder and imagination. Early primitive people heard each rock and bush and brook speak with meaning, but we have "hushed the bushes and gagged the rocks."

Creation affirms the Creator. The wisdom tradition is a way of seeing and being in the world, affirming the blessings of God in creation and suggesting that nature itself is a manifestation of God. The spirit of the divine is the breath within us. Thus, we recognize ourselves as one with nature and take incarnation seriously. The universe is the Thought of God, the Action of Christ and the Power of the Spirit. Israel through its wisdom literature recognized the unity between Creator and creation.

Job asked, demanded, that he speak face to face with God, and that God answer his questions concerning justice. God was silent for thirty-nine chapters, but at the climax of the story God answered Job out of a whirlwind, telling him to look at creation.

11. A celebration of wonder. To wonder is to be open to surprise and possibility. It is the source of gratitude, expectancy, and trust, a necessary quality of an authentic and abundant life, the attitude of awareness of the holy. It bridges the gulf between the sacred and secular, extraordinary and ordinary, church and world, history and nature, faith and reason, spirit and body, and heaven and earth. Wonder is the willingness to see the common in a uncommon way.

Abraham Heschel the Jewish mystic and professor of ethics wrote, "Wonder alone is the compass that may direct us to the pole of meaning."[14] We do not create the ineffable, we encounter it.

Acts of wonder are symbols of the meaning for which all things stand. We are beings in quest of meaning. Why is there a world? Why is there a me? What is the meaning of what happens, of what I do, and who I am? Why am I here?

Wonder is a gift from God, making wise the simple (Psalm 19:7):

> The simple in heart see things
> The wise may never know,
> The wonder of the winter
> In soft, small flakes of snow,
> The new life in the springtime,
> The magic of the tree,
> The splendor of the sunlight
> In summer on the sea,

The glory of the autumn...
They never wait to worship until
They understand these mysteries,
Because... they know they never will.

The poet Wallace Stevens wrote in one of his essays on reality and the imagination: "The philosopher proves that the philosopher exists. The poet merely enjoys existence."

12. <u>Personified as a woman,</u> a feminine presence with God, to be a guide to the people. In Hebrew Wisdom is "Hokmah" and in Greek, "Sophia".

What if life is a banquet
     and you and I refuse the invitation
     to eat the bread and wine and
     be merry in God's place?

What if life is a game
     and you and I refuse to choose
     the invitation to God's grace?

What if wisdom is a love affair with learning?

The wisdom approach to learning from the Book of Job includes <u>choosing</u>. Choose from the following those that would fit the interests of your particular class:

1. In Robert Fulghum's <u>All I Really Need To Know I Learned In Kindergarten,</u>[15] one of his pieces of wisdom is : Take a nap every afternoon. He suggests that it would be a better world if we all had cookies and milk about three o'clock every afternoon and then lay down with our blankies for a nap. In your imagination picture warring dictators and soldiers, business executives and hungry, homeless, street people sitting down together with warm cookies and cold milk and blankies for taking a nap. After your imaging, write your symbols for "cookies" and "warm, soft blankies," symbols of security and food for the spirit.

Discuss: Is there only one answer—theological orthodoxy? What is "theological orthodoxy"? Whose "orthodoxy"?

2. Read and discuss the following story and how it is related to wisdom theology:

A very wise man taught his students from an inexhaustible store of wisdom. All his knowledge was in a thick tome which he allowed no one to open. When the scholar died, his students were anxious to possess his knowledge and ran to open the book. They were very surprised, confused, disappointed. There was only one page. On it was written: "When you realize the difference between the container and the content, you will have knowledge."[16]

Reflect in silence on what the story is saying to you.

3. Discuss in small groups or the entire class, depending on the size and preference of the participants: What religious convictions you held as a child have changed for you?

4. Discuss Penny's story and your own in relationship to failure. Does God "answer" prayers? Give reasons, or better still, experiences, for your response. How do we discover the "will of God"? What do you think is God's will for you?

5. Recall the story of Jesus' life. Did Jesus ever fail? The wisdom tradition also acknowledges that there are paradoxes in life rather than one "right" answer. "Yes" and "no." Give your thoughts and feelings and be open to the opinions and experiences of others, for we can learn from wise persons, as well as from our own experience.

6. Recall the story of Job. What happened to Job? Why? Who are the characters in the story? Why did Job protest to God? How did the story end? Did Job win or lose, in your opinion? Read chapter 28:12.

7. Close with singing a song from your hymnal that emphasizes trust in God or the mystery of God, and prayer.

Bibliography:

Robert Alter. The Art of Biblical Poetry, "Truth and Poetry in the Book of Job" (New York: Basic Books, 1985) pp. 85-110.

Brueggmann, Walter. The Creative World (Philadelphia: Fortress Press, 1989)

Frost, Robert. "A Masque of Reason" from Complete Poems of Robert Frost (New York: Henry Holt, 1949), p. 596.

Edwin Good, In Turns Of Tempest (Stanford, Cal: Stanford University, 1990).

Habel, Norman C. Job (Atlanta: John Knox Press, 1981).

Melchert, Charles F. "Wisdom is Vindicated by Her Deeds," *Religious Education,* Vol 87, No. 1, Winter, 1992.

Terrien, Samuel. Job: The Poet of Existence (Indianapolis: Bobbs-Merrill, 1957).

[1] John Wilcox, The Bitterness of Job: A Philosophical Reading (Ann Arbor: University of Michigan Press, 1989).

[2] Charles Melchert, Lancaster Theological Seminary, June 1992.

[3] Jurgen Moltmann, Theology of Play (New York: Harper & Row, 1972) p. 20.

[4] Edward Hays, "The Wedding Gift" St. George & the Dragon (Easton, KS: Forest of Peace Books) p. 51.

[5] Penny Defore, "The Failure That Helped Me Grow Up," The Guideposts Christmas Treasury, p. 87.

[6] Fred Craddock, As One Without Authority (Nashville, Abingdon, 1987).

[7] Ibid., p. 7

[8] Ibid., p. 11

[9] Ibid., p. 13

[10] Ibid., p. 14

[11] Larry Dossey, Space, Time & Medicine (Boulder, Shambhala, 1982).

[12] Mel Ellis, Sermons in Stones, (New York: Holt, Rinehart & Winston, 1975).

[13] Annie Dillard, Pilgrim at Tinker Creek (New York: Bantam, 1982).

[14] Abraham Joshua Heschel, Man is Not Alone: A Philosophy of Religion (New York: The Noonday Press, 1991).

[15] Robert Fulghum, All I Really Need to Know I Learned in Kindergarten (NY: Villard Books, 1988).

[16] Indries Shah, Contrary to Expectation, The Book of Books (New York: Octagon, 1969).

ASH WEDNESDAY

Suggested format: This is merely a suggested outline, for there is more material in each session than you will be able to cover in an hour's session, if you involve the group in activities.

(10 minutes) Brainstorm with the group: What do you recall of the Job story?
(10 minutes) Tell the story of Job and discuss it.
(15 minutes) Tell "The Riddle of Existence" and discuss it.
(10 minutes) Share "The Scream," "I Am Rowing" and write a prayer of confession
(10 minutes) Story "Mr. Gold" and "That is Enough."
(5 minutes) Close with ashes, hymn, and prayer.

"Is this all?" "Job...sat among the ashes" (2:8).

Part 1

Ask participants to list the characters, as they recall the story from their memories and any other details not included in the story recorded here. Write key words on the board. What is the conflict?

Once upon a time there lived a man who had a large and happy family, a big farm and many cattle. He feared and loved God, helped and took care of his neighbors, for God had blessed him. His name was Job.

One day God and Satan were talking together and Satan said, "Your servants serve you because you reward them. Take away a person's family and property and health and see what happens."

Satan was very persuasive and so God said, "All right. Test Job."

So Job's cattle died, his sons and daughters died, his friends, all but three, left him, and his body was covered with sores. He sat in dust and ashes, in misery, and his three friends sat with him in silence in the ashheap.

To be in ashes is to experience the wound of being human.

Old Mr. Gold, sinking beneath his sadness, asked Jacob the Baker, "Tell me, Jacob. It this it? Is this all? Is there nothing more?

The poet of the book of Job, attempting to answer that question as he faced the crisis of faith, the riddle of existence, the meaning of life and suffering, continued the story of Job, stripped of all his possessions and honor, symbolically put to death, asking, "Is this the meaning of existence? Is there nothing more?

The book of Job is both a folktale and a poem. Chapters 1 and 2 (the beginning of the story) and 42:7-17 (the ending) are written in prose. Chapters 3-42 are poetic commentary on the parable.

The folktale is ancient. Although we cannot be sure of the date of the composition of the book, it reads as if Israel were in exile, the Temple destroyed, and therefore the covenant with Yahweh broken. The poet's theology (that God rewards the good and punishes the evil) no longer fits his experience. The Book of Job is a writing from the wisdom tradition.

Job sat in the ashheap of his sorrow and suffering and asked, "What is the meaning of existence. Is this all there is?"

All of us search for the meaning of existence, the riddle of life, but when we are in deep agony, all we do is feel its horror. Job sat in the ashes and suffered his riddle on earth.

Reflect and discuss: What does the story do to or for you? Do you think there is such a thing as "disinterested piety"? Why do you tithe, teach Sunday School, attend worship, feed the hungry?

Part 2

If you have not used the overall view of the wisdom tradition in the Introduction, you may wish to spend some time in lecture on the wisdom tradition (see p.7).

Ash Wednesday begins the season of Lent, reminding us of brokenness and humility. Jesus came so that we might have abundant life. He became the channel of that abundant life to his Master's world.

The Pharisees lived by the Law. They knew who God was and what God willed, for God's laws for living were clear to them and they felt comfortable in that knowledge. Then entered the Stranger, a humble preacher, a carpenter from Nazareth, who healed on the Sabbath.

"It is a sin!" "It is against the Law of our fathers!" "On the Sabbath we rest!" The Pharisees were furious.

James looked questioningly at Jesus. "Master, I am sorry. I was so hungry. You know how long we have been healing the people." James began to explain and apologize for eating on the Sabbath.

"Shhh, James. It is all right." Jesus put his hand on his disciple's arm. He spoke calmly. "I was the one who told you you could eat. Let me speak."

Before Jesus could speak, however, the Pharisees shouted, "You cannot heal on the Sabbath!"

Jesus looked into the frightened faces of his disciples. They did not know what to say or do. He looked into the angry faces of the Pharisees who lived by these rules. "If you had a sheep or an oxen and it fell into a hole on the Sabbath, would you help it out and save it?"

Jesus' disciples nodded their heads in agreement. The Pharisees, however, frowned. They were silent as they waited for Jesus to continue.

"A person is more important than a sheep. You preach God's word on the Sabbath. We do God's will on the Sabbath, for God wants all creation to be well and whole."

The Pharisees stared at Jesus with hatred. He had not only broken their holy laws, he had made his own law of love sound right. "We must stop this man," they said among themselves. And they plotted to kill Jesus.

Ash Wednesday is the recognition of our plots to silence Christ in our lives, for as Jesus overthrew the values and practices of his day, he threatens our established beliefs today, as well. He tells how God breaks into our lives, revealing our illusions so that we may face the reality of God's love that transcends all our failures, successes, sins, and even our assurances, so that we may experience forgiveness.

On Ash Wednesday we mourn. We mourn over the havoc wrought by the four horsemen of the Apocalypse: Power, War, Famine, and Death. We mourn over rituals uncreated, especially rituals needed when we remember those who have not spoken, rituals that enable us to mourn beyond frail words so tears may flow freely, not to be ashamed of, for imaginations left unused, limited by what the society thinks and says. We mourn over the lack of peace and justice in our world. Jesus cried over Jerusalem, the symbol of the world's devotion to power and weapons, fear and security.

Allan Boesak wrote of seeing young people with nothing in their hands, marching in the streets to say, "We want to share with you our anguish for the future of this country we shall inherit, a country where we shall not be safe, where we shall not be able to live as human beings together. Let us change that." He concluded: "And I saw those young persons teargassed; I saw them shot down with rifles."

The psalmist cried, "How long must I bear pain in my soul, and have sorrow in my heart all the day?" (Psalm 13:2) Where one child suffers, we all suffer. When one suffers, God suffers most.

Lent is a time of weeping, a time to cry. In this place we cry our prayers to God, who collects our tears.

Ash Wednesday is a call for preparation for reconciliation, as well. Jesus came to baptize us with the Holy Spirit as we commit our lives to Christ. It is not easy to walk through flames, to burn in the fire, to shed the masks and skins of the world, to be transformed into a new creature.

The phoenix rises from the ashes, as the new life only comes out of the death of the old. Fire illuminates, warms, and purifies. There is need for fire that purifies and purges.

Because we care, we wonder why leaders in Third World countries, seeing the dire plight of their people, cheat them, as we enjoy the aroma and taste of coffee grown in their fields, picked by peasants with parched throats and empty stomachs.

I remember the day I heard the preacher's words on South Africa and the feelings overwhelmed the words. "How could any people so abuse and harm the people on whose land they lived? What can I do?"

The frustration mounted and when I left, I simply walked and walked, without knowing where I was walking. I was overwhelmed with a sense of hopelessness and then I was angry. "How could such injustice be allowed in the world. What was I doing?"

The title of the talk was "The Pervasiveness of Evil and the Persistence of Grace." All I heard, however, was the pervasiveness of evil.

It was not until three days later, I heard the rest of the title, for the speaker had also told of how the people under oppression, who owned nothing, whose lives where as cheap as the sands of their land, loved and supported one another with all that they had. They were people with a cause and a faith. Someday they would be free. It was a matter of time. They were not hopeless and they were not helpless. They believed they were doing the will of God.

This Ash Wednesday, as we look at the world, hear its cries, we want to be God, to comfort and to cure. However, we are not God.

On the third day I heard the preacher's last words, as he told of his experience of visiting the Fore Trekker Monument in Pretoria with his son, looking out at the skyline of Pretoria, surrounded by a circle of wagons, symbolizing the implacability of the white South African to dominate and stay.

In contrast he recalled the colorful felt banner in Johannesberg; people bringing gifts to Jesus, gifts of peace, and he concluded, "It is my religious faith that trusts that God's grace is even stronger than the Four Trekkers Monument."

Discuss the meaning of "wisdom" by exploring participants' meaning. Whom do you call a "wise person"? What does one do with experience that does not fit the community's teaching? What is the place of experience? of tradition? of Scripture? of reason?

List on paper as many "wise" people as you can think of. Include contemporaries and people you know personally. Then brainstorm with the entire group.

On Ash Wednesday we cry. In a world of need and lack, where 3/4 of the people go to bed hungry every night, where 5% of the population owns 35% of the wealth, where the unemployed, handicapped, abused, gay, lay, Native American, refugee, black, children, women, minorities, have become victims, it is time to speak and listen to prophetic voices from the past and present. It is time for justice, peace, liberation, healing, and hope.

And Jesus stood up to read:

"The Spirit of the Lord is on me, because he has anointed me to preach good news to the poor. He has sent me to proclaim freedom for the prisoners and recovery of sight for the blind, to release the oppressed, to proclaim the year of the Lord's favor." (Luke 4:18,19)

Jesus ministered to the "anawim," the forgotten and oppressed ones. When the rich man went away sorrowing because he could not give up his wealth, they asked Jesus, "Who then can be saved?" Jesus replied, "What is impossible with men is possible with God."

As Christians we read and hear the story of the Israelites in bondage in Egypt under the oppressor Pharaoh and we know instinctively that this is wrong. "The Lord said, 'I have indeed seen the misery of my people in Egypt. I have heard them crying out because of their slave drivers and I am concerned about their suffering." (Exodus 3:7)

We know it is wrong because we believe that all are created in the image of God and no one should be a slave to another. Most of us have grown up with freedom and "liberty for all," although not at all times. Those of us who have grown up the Christian church are aware of the evil and fight in varying ways for the "underdog," the one who is powerless and bound.

On Ash Wednesday we read the psalms that speak of God's concern for the oppressed: "(God) will defend the afflicted among the people and save the children of the needy; he will crush the oppressor." (Psalm 72:4)

And when the Israelites, released from their bondage, in turn became the oppressor, the Lord spoke out against the people. God is more concerned with justice than with privilege. "I hate, I despise your religious feasts; I cannot stand your assemblies." (Amos 5:2l) "And what does the Lord require of you?" God's messenger, Micah asks: "To act justly and to love mercy and to walk humbly with your God. (6:8)

Then I saw a new heaven and a new earth, for the first heaven and the first earth had passed away,.." (Revelation 21:1) We too look forward to a new heaven and a new earth, the home of righteousness, where justice will be at home.

Yet a new birth does not come without the pangs of labor, the terror of transformation, the cost of courage and sacrifice.

Look around, the world is full of hopelessness. Our cities are dying, choking to death with smog and pollution, crime and violence, our lakes are dying and so our forests. People are dying in vicious wars or poverties, in the clutches of cancer or loneliness. And even the dying of vision and hope.

The poets of Job used a story: "There was once a man in the land of Uz whose name was Job..." and this story helps us face honestly the events of our lives and the lives of suffering people around the world whose "service is hard on earth," with months of emptiness, nights of misery, and days without hope.

The book of Job is a story that takes place anywhere, anytime. God and Satan debate Job's motivation for fearing God. "Does Job fear God for nothing?" asked Satan. Is there such a thing as disinterested piety? God gives Job into the power of Satan, who takes from him his possessions, servants, and sons and daughters, his reputation. Yet Job is innocent and out of his suffering, pain, and innocence asks, "Why do bad things happen to good people?" What kind of God can allow the torture of the innocent? It is the questions asked during and after the Holocaust. It is the question we ask out of our own experiences with suffering.

This upright man became a model of suffering, a brother to all sufferers and his story allowed the poets, using an ancient folktale, to ask their questions of the prevailing traditional theology of their time.

Bewildered, alone, in misery and doubt, Job represents all of us in our darkest hours of despair.

Complete "Evil is..." List "evils" in your home, church, community, world and brainstorm possible ways to respond.

Discuss: What "color," "race," or "class" is Jesus for you?

List some of the injustices of which you are aware of around the world. Discuss them one by one, determining on the basis of what you know the degree of their injustice and why. If there are issues on which there is lack of information, assign volunteers to study and make a report on them for the next meeting. List the prophets of justice and peace past and present.

The poet William Yeats wrote in his poem, 'The Second Coming': "Things fall apart; the center cannot hold;.."

Job's world was overturned. His possessions and family were destroyed and he was left crying his anguish to God. I wonder what Job would have said to the poet? As Job questioned God, crying out for the justice of defending himself, of knowing the identity of his guilt, would he perhaps have stated the above as a question: "When things fall part, can the center hold?"

"Go away," Job pleaded to God. "Let me suffer and die in peace." When things fall apart solitude becomes angonizing loneliness, abandonment by friends and God. Hospitality becomes hostility. Even the cosmos seems to be against us. Yet, if prayer is communication with God, Job never lost God, for when all else was gone, Job prayed, and though he may not have been aware of it, he kept his "center."

Because he was honest, he did not pray a prayer of thanksgiving (except in the prose introduction: The Lord gives and the Lord takes away, blessed be the Lord!), nor praise, nor intercession, nor even confession, for Job was a blameless man. He petitioned God, demanding justice, out of his suffering and his anger.

Perhaps we might say, "When we no longer trust the center, God, things fall apart." Yeats' poem continues: "Mere anarchy is loosed upon the world." It feels today, when we watch television and read the newspaper, that anarchy is loosed upon our world. And, returning to Job, we ask, "Does one have to lose all hope in human props in order, at last, to receive God's grace alone?"

Chuck Melchert, teaching a class on the book of Job, asked, "Do we dare, in our congregations, to engage our people's passions in their educational ministry (in our preaching)? Do we dare touch their bodies and their sores in the process of learning God?"

Job helps us reflect upon God and God's participation in the world and in our lives.

Yeats continued:
"The blood-dimmed tide is loosed, and everywhere
The ceremony of innocence is drowned;
The best lack all conviction, while the worst
Are full of passionate intensity."

"Job's speeches are passionate because theology cannot be reduced to cool intellect—it rises from and engages with our whole being," Melchert states. "It is full of passion, because our passions show us what we are most devoted to, what we have a passion for...Job's passion is God-and he knows that passion in every fibre of his being."

Because we know the pain and tears of the third world we have come to this place not only to confess that we have not shared in their suffering but to seek an answer to why the world must suffer so, for all of us are dis-eased and "near death." Many have come to seek a refuge from the brutality of a world that seems immune to the cries of its people. We seek love and forgiveness, courage and value, even joy in this place, for all of us bear the wound of being human.

We live in an age of compromise. Let us not think otherwise or deny it. As we recognize and confess it, we are given forgiveness and courage to live with the ambiguities, paradoxes, and evils of our world. There are tragic failures.

The story of Job is our story. It is a symbolic story or metaphor that stands for the suffering of all people exposed to the evils of being human and fallible. This is a drama of the divinity of God and the humanity of Job.

All of us search for the meaning of existence, the riddle of life, but when we are in deep agony, all we do is feel its horror. Job sat in the ashes and suffered his riddle on earth.

Part 3

Tell or read the story "The Riddle of Existence":

Lady Zane and her friends reached the edge of existence and stopped to try to figure out what was happening. "It's important," said Lady Zane. "There must be something more to existence than this. Is this all there is to it?"

The travelers were baffled, disappointed, and exhausted. They had come to a wall, an empty space, a question mark. What does one do before a wall, or emptiness, or the question of existence?

Lady Zane thought for a while. "It is a riddle," she said, at last. "The Riddle of Existence. We must create something. We can only move forward into something new by creating it."

"But God has already created everything!" Nasja exclaimed.

"It's part of the game," said Lady Zane. "God wants us to create."

Lady Zane by responding to the questions of her friends was coming closer to the Riddle. "By creating something you move into the empty space, and thus deeper into existence."

But she did not know how. Whether by prayer or pretending, faith or believing, she was not sure. She knew, however, that is would be fun. "You don't think about it. You must do it."

Then came the excuses: "I'm tired." "I don't feel creative," and the complaints.

To show she understood or was willing to risk on what little she

29

understood, Lady Zane moved into the blank space and the others went with her and something new occurred.

Precisely at the intersection between God and the travelers, the Riddle of Existence was posed and answered, and the chase was able to continue for a little while longer.[1]

Reflect on the story, "The Riddle of Existence." Discuss: What does the story say to you? Is life a riddle? Part of a game? Does God want us to create? What? Why? How? Is that fun for you? What are your excuses? What do you think was the "something new" that occurred? What do you do when you are at "the edge of existence"?

Job, perplexed and suffering, sits among the ashes and three of his friends come to sit with him for seven days and nights in silence. Job's friends provided the traditional answer of Israel, the covenantal relationship with Yahweh in which the good prosper and the evil suffer. But Israel had been in exile and her experience did not fit the formula.

His friends gave Job, as many Western missionaries used to give the "natives," a theology divorced from their situation. "Here is tradition, now make your life fit it."

Job looked at his experience and had the courage to say, "Here is my life. It doesn't fit the tradition. I must change my theology."

I spent three years every Saturday morning memorizing catechism: the traditional heritage and beliefs of my denomination. We learned with our intellect. We had the words. We talked about God. We learned by hearsay from a past that was dead. The pastor asked a question. We regurgitated an answer.

The tragedy was not that he taught us the wrong words. The tragedy was how he showed us to live the answers. He refused communion to the mother of my best friend because she was divorced.

I longed for grace and he gave me law.

I longed for love and he gave me a harsh and just God.

I longed for experiencing the joy of communing with God and he gave me traditional talk about God.

I needed the wonder of the grandeur of God within and a new wisdom in creation, the sense of wonder that leads us to reconciliation with ourself and with our Creator.

Job is the poet of existence. He traveled beyond the ignorance and arrogance of religion, for Job learned from active contemplation of God's creativity. He discovered the meaning of existence in the miracle of creativity.

Job stood up to God, questioned God, for the sake of the truth. Job wanted to know what the charges were against him because he believed in righteousness being rewarded and unrighteousness being punished.

The book of Job is a way of looking at life creatively, for our task is to live forward, create life, to make of it what it is not yet, and to reflect on it backward.

A friend told me of his ten-year-old daughter who like Huck Finn "gave up" on prayer. It seems that God gave her no answer, like Job. "If God won't talk to me," she said, "then I won't talk to God."

The ten-year-old did ask her father, "When does God talk to you?" and he told her, what God told Job. He pointed to creation.

Life is a riddle. It calls for discernment, prayer, communion, rather than cognitive answers.

God answered as Jesus did, before Pilate's question, "What is truth?" Jesus stood before Pilate in silence.

Is this all? We seek answers out of deep longing and searching, out of the pain of being human, out of the agony of suffering.

Lent reminds us of Jesus' suffering, beginning with Ash Wednesday. Ashes are the sign of repentence and forgiveness. They are as frail and silent as a moth's wings. Thus a symbol of our frailty and brokenness, a symbol of our silence.

Part 4

A piece of sculpture at the Yad Vashem Holocaust Museum in Jerusalem is entitled "The Scream." Shirley Samberg has created a figure suggesting a person. Black fabric and clay covers a pole with arms stretched upward, stopping at the neck, for there is no head, no face, no voice. The absence of a mouth is the silent scream, pleading to a heaven of hope or an absent, silent God. It is a symbol for the voiceless, for those without freedom or justice. Job pleaded for justice. The Third World cries out for justice. All of us have experienced our dream and desire for justice.

The sculpture said to me that we are given a choice to love or to fear, to trust God and work for peace and justice, or out of fear to use violence and power. It is the war of myths. Jesus tells us one story. The world tells us another. We are fighting for narrative space.

That sculpture also says to me that we need a Savior to lift us from the ashes of our despair and sense of hopelessness, and we need a people who will follow that Savior, willing to speak for those without a face or a voice. It is the call to be that absent voice, that silent heaven, to speak God's word of love and forgiveness to a waiting, suffering world.

As the artist sculptured with her material, the poet sculptures with her words, both revealing Ash Wednesday living:

> I am rowing, I am rowing
> Though the oarlocks stick and are rusty
> And the sea blinks and rolls...
> I am rowing, I am rowing
> Though the wind pushes me back
> And I know that the island will not be perfect
> It will have the flaws of life...
> But there will be a door
>   and I will open it
> And I will get rid of the rat inside of me,
> The gnawing, pestilential rat.
> God will take it with his two hands
> And embrace it."[2]

God embraces the rat that will rid us from its living within us, but Christianity does not offer a cheap, simple answer.

Paul knew evil and suffering and wrote of the good that he would do and did not. As we look at our weed infested garden, the world, the "rat" gnaws deeper. As we look at poverty and suspicion and nuclear tension around the world, in our own backyard or livingroom, we know it is only God who can "take it with two hands and embrace it."

When our eyes are opened to the despair, destruction, death of our brothers and sisters in Central America, South Africa, India, Palestine, around the world, with the Job's who suffer, we become aware of the needs of others and confess our sinfulness, our brokenness, and pray for strength, forgiveness, and solidarity with those who suffer. We pray also for the wisdom required to live with Job and Jesus this Lenten season.

Part 5

> Mr. Gold continued, "Jacob, where do you find the strength to carry on in life?"
>
> Jacob replied that life is often heavy because we attempt to carry it. "But I do find a strength in the ashes."
>
> In the ashes?" asked Mr. Gold
>
> Yes," said Jacob, "for each of us is alone. And each of us is on a journey. In the process of our journey, we must bend to build a fire for light, and warmth, and food. But when our fingers tear at the ground, hoping to find the coals of another's fire, what we often find are the ashes. The ashes will not give us warmth or light, but testimony. Because these ashes tell us that somebody else has been in the night, somebody else has bent to build a fire, and somebody else has carried on. And that can be enough, sometimes.[3]

Reflect on Jacob the baker's words in the story above. The gospel of Jesus Christ is "good news," not "happy talk." What does it mean to you?

Discuss Jesus' words, "In the world you have tribulation; but be of good cheer, I have overcome the world" (John 16:33) and sing triumphantly "In Christ There Is No East or West" and "For All the Saints." Pray a prayer for peace, justice, freedom from oppression, poverty, and evil, or: "I know that I read the gospel through my insular lenses. Loan me, O homeless black, dying brown Salvadorean, poor white woman, hungry yellow child, new lenses. In Christ's name. Amen."

Ashes are a symbol of suffering and of solidarity. The Christian of old saw in the ashes of the phoenix new life rising out of death, and Jesus came to baptize us with the Holy Spirit as we commit our new lives to God's purposes, assured of the power of that Spirit to enable us to live that life. It is not easy to live this commitment, to walk through flames of fire, to shed the masks and skins of the world, in order to be transformed into a new creature. Sometimes, with Jacob the Baker, we feel the ashes can be enough. There are other times, however, I cry out for more, for the story of Lent, of Jesus' passion through which I know Christ understands my pain because he sat in the ashheap and suffered.

Today we burn last year's palm leaves to make the ashes that are placed on our foreheads as the symbol of Christ's resurrection from the ashheap. For me <u>that</u> is "enough."

Tell or read the story "That Is Enough":

People were sitting around asking him questions. His answers were so beautiful. When the others had run out of questions, there was a long silence. Then I heard myself asking, "What do I need to know?"

He didn't answer. Just kept looking at me—for several minutes. Tears began to run down his cheek. But he looked happy enough.

Someone nudged me. "Ask him another question."

No," he said. "that's the best question. I was thinking of the time I asked that very question of my master—when I first entered the monastery, fifty years ago. I will tell you how my master answered. He told me to take that question, 'What do I need to know?' and put it to every single monk. I did. Then he had me sit in solitude for a year, reflecting on their answers. Next he had me find a ship and sail around the world, putting my question to everyone I met. That took me six years. And I had to reflect on the answers in solitude for six years. That's how my master answered my question."

The room became silent again. "But Sir," I insisted, "please, what do I need to know?"

Good," he answered. "I will give you—Christ, and that will be enough."[4]

This day we wear ashes on our foreheads, remembering that "ashes to ashes and dust to dust" is our destiny...except...with God all things are possible!

Part 6

Place ashes on the foreheads of those who come forward during the singing of a hymn.

Choose from Additional Activities:

Guided faith meditation: Close your eyes. Place your feet on the floor and your hands on your lap. Relax. Take a deep breath. You are in your imagination in your home. You can smell your favorite food cooking on the stove. You can feel your mother or your father's arms around you and hear them telling you that they love you. (Pause) Suddenly you sniff, the smells turn sour. You are very angry and hurt. You think, "It isn't fair!" as you recall something that has happened to you that was not fair. You decide to tell God (or Jesus) about it. Put your feelings into words. You can say whatever you feel, because to get rid of bad feelings we must put them into words. (Pause) You take a deep breath because it feels good that it is outside of you and not inside anymore. Then you are quiet, for God is telling you what to do. (Pause)

Give thanks and take a deep breath. It is good to be alive. It is good to forgive, to let go of a hurt, and be forgiven. Go back to your favorite room again and do one of the things you like best to do. (Pause) Then slowly open your eyes when you are ready and return to this place.

Ask for volunteers to read the following passages aloud and discuss their meaning: I Samuel 2:8a, Luke 1:52-53, Matthew 12:18-21, Acts 5:29, Ephesians 4:24, I Corinthians 4:20, Mark 2:22, Daniel 3:18.

Write letters of support for individuals and groups working for the causes of justice, peace, and freedom. Write letters through Amnesty International.

Assignment: Read and reflect Chapter 3 of Job.

[1]Based on Emilie Griffin, Chasing the Kingdom: A Parable of Faith (San Francisco: Harper Collins, 1990).
[2]Anne Sexton, The Awful Rowing Toward God
[3]Noah ben Shea, Jacob the Baker (New York: Ballantine Books, 1982) p. 112.
[4]Theophane the Monk, Tales of a Magic Monastery (N.Y: Crossroad, 1981).

Session Two

A REASONABLE ROARING

Suggested format:
(10 minutes) Job's anger
(10 minutes) Story: Four-year-old's death of father
(15 minutes) Story: Davida Angelica
(10 minutes) Story: Mother's anger
(10 minutes) All wounded: two films, end of four-year-old's story
(5 minutes) Close with hymn, prayer of confession, words of assurance

"After this Job opened his mouth and cursed the day of his birth... roarings poured out like waters" (Job 3:1, 24).

Part 1

We come to the book of Job, our ears stuffed with the story of Job's "patience." But listen to the words: "After this Job opened his mouth and cursed the day of his birth" (3:l). So begins Job's protest.

Job does not take his suffering patiently, for it is not deserved. His question is the question we ask today, listening to and looking at the world around us: "Why do the innocent suffer? Why do bad things happen to good people? Where is God? Doesn't God care?"

The poetry, chapters 3-42, was written during a time of trouble and torment. Israel was in exile. What had happened to her covenant relationship with God? Job's question was her question.

Job's opening soliloquy is a string of curses. He asks for death and curses life, not God, although he accuses God. Given the tensions and horrors of today, I think it likely that all of us have experienced Job's wrath and confusion, his crisis of faith and trust in a loving, merciful God.

Without an awareness of what this story is doing, without understanding that chapters I-2 and the end of 42 is an ancient folktale, a "set-up: for the poetry (3-42) to create a new theology in which God does not reward the good and punish the evil, without this awareness, we built a theology of "blame God."

Job reminds me of our relatives Adam and Eve. "She (Eve) did it!" "The snake did it." "It's your fault, God, you are omniscient and omnipotent."

His friends give advice. "You have sinned, Job. Repent."

We, the hearers/readers of the story know, however, that the "adversary" has challenged "disinterested piety."

Job's words border on blasphemy, but when we read them "in the pit," in the depths of despair, they ring true and honest. Job is a man of integrity.

The book of Job is a story of paradox, of contradictions and ambiguity. On the one hand no one is an island. On the other hand..Job found himself alone, set adrift on a sea of suffering, with friends who lectured instead of listened and a God who would not answer. It is the story of one who defended his integrity and raged "against the dying of the light" vs surrender of the self, trust in the absolute love of God. It is the story of doubt whose core is trust, absolute faith in the One at whom he is roaring.

"Cursed be the day I was born," Job roared. "God damn my birthday!"

Discuss Job's anger.

Part 2

Anger is the first stage of grief. Repressed anger eats from within. A friend of mine conducts "wonded healers" weekend retreats. Attending one, I observed the rest of our small group do their "work," share their wounds, and wondered how vulnerable I was. There was no forced confession, but when the time was right, we each felt comfortable to reveal our needs and tell our story.

Tell or read the story:

> They climbed the stairs wearily, heavy with the truth they were delivering. Their knock was loud and impatient, angry as the echo of their message.
>
> The four-year-old child looked up from her play to watch her mother cross the room. She listened to the murmurs of the sad voices filling the corners with their sorrow, and then her mother's cries.
>
> Although she did not hear it that night, the message the police pronounced was her father's death. He was killed immediately as the car he was driving in return for the new car he had just delivered, catapaulted into the passing train, for it had no brakes.
>
> Just as quickly she was hurtled into God's arms, her adopted Father, although she did not know it then. How could she know, when her church taught her that God was an angry judge.
>
> That "father" she rejected, for there still was a flickering flame of remembrance of her daddy's love.
>
> As she grew, she searched for her absent parent, for do we not all project upon God the image of our human parents? And having been taught to think rather than feel, she was unaware that the absent parents, both the human one and the divine, were with her all along.
>
> Her search led her years later to a seminary a second time, a second chance, and there God approached her in the form of a woman, a healer of wounded healers.
>
> "What do I do now?" I asked, after "doing my work."
>
> "I think you have repressed your anger over your wounds. Let it out. God can take it. God loves you."

"Cursed be the day I was born," Job roared.

"Cursed be the day my father was killed," I roared, and in the roaring I remembered a story of Davida Angelica.

Part 3

There once was a lioness whose name was Davida Angelica. Everybody called her Angel. Angel didn't roar very often. In fact, she had only roared once in her life.

It was when she was just a little cub. She was playing in the grass with her brothers and sisters, and a hunter's arrow pierced her shoulder. Angel roared in surprise and her mother chased the hunter away.

Angel's mother tried to pull the arrow out, but the shaft broke off and the arrow point stayed in Angel's shoulder. It hurt when she walked, but in time the wound healed at the surface and Angel forgot all about what happened. Everyone else forgot too.

The only reminder Angel had of the wounding was the pain in her shoulder. But after a while, she hardly noticed it. And when she did feel the pain, she thought that all lions felt that way.

Angel grew up to be one of the favorite lions in the forest. She was gentle and kind. By the time she was a young lioness on her first hunt, she had forgotten all about the wounding. But even when she made her first kill, she did not roar like the other lions.

One day, as Angel was hunting food for her own cubs, she noticed a pain in her shoulder. She thought to herself, "What is that feeling? Have I felt it before?"

Soon the pain began to grow. Angel's shoulder hurt when she jumped out of trees or carried her cubs or ran fast to catch a deer. After several months, Angel's shoulder hurt all the time. She began to limp and her hunting suffered because she could not run fast enough. Finally, she could not move at all.

The wise ones came from far and near to gather around her. They brought food for her cubs, healing herbs, and stories of the great hunters. They surrounded her with warmth and breathed strong breaths with her. Their growls swirled around her and under her, and wrapped her like a mantle of fire.

That night as the moon rose, Angel herself began to growl. At first it was a low growl, and when she raised her head, the pain stabbed through her. Then she growled a low roar. And a bigger roar. And then the growls of the wise ones lifted her to her feet and she began to ROAR.

Davida Angelica roared and roared and roared. All the lowly animals shivered in their beds. Davida Angelica roared and roared and roared and the fur on her shoulder began to split. Davida Angelica roared and roared and roared and the skin under the fur popped open and yellow liquid poured out of her shoulder. The liquid gathered in a pool on the ground, and in the middle of the pool was an arrow point. Davida Angelica roared and roared and roared and roared. And then she was quiet.

The wise ones looked at the arrow point, growled, and nodded, for now they remembered and understood. And then the oldest one said, "Davida Angelica, from this day forward, you will be called Davida. You have lived through a wounding. You have survived great pain with courage. You will be called Davida the Courageous. Davida with the Roar that Heals.

Then the wise ones roared. And Davida roared with them. And they all roared long into the night.[1]

Job roared to a living God.

Angel roared to a living God.

And in our struggle to become human, there are times we roar to a living God together, for that is what Christian community is all about—our relationship with God together.

Reflect and discuss what the story said to you. Do you believe that "roars heal"? Have you ever been wounded and healed? What was the source of the healing? Was Job's roaring appropriate or "sinful"? Did Jesus ever "roar"? Against what did Jesus rage? Against what or whom do you rage?

The deepest realities are paradoxical. Anger is one of them. On the one hand anger and letting go can cause harm. On the other hand it can create forgiveness and healing. Anger must be expressed or it will fester with destructive results.

Part 4

The mother was afraid of anger. The church had taught her that anger was evil, sinful, and having cut her teeth on the words of the book of James, all her life she had pretended that she was not angry.

She had never roared even though the arrow points pierced her heart. She did not roar her hurt when her young husband was killed and she was left to care for their four-year-old daughter alone, during the depression years. She was helpless but she was not "angry," when the insurance company went bankrupt because of the depression, and after his death she was left penniless. Instead, she had a nervous breakdown.

Because she was afraid of anger, her daughter was not allowed to be angry either.

They lived together in two small rooms. The landlady, and her daughter of the same age, lived in the same house, but only one of the daughters was allowed to be angry at the other.

"I'm sorry that it's not fair and she takes advantage of you, but if you get angry, we will have to move."

Whether the mother never let the sun go down on her wrath, I do not know, but I do know that anger, locked up, seeks revenge.

Her anger became heavy and made the mother tired.

Anger scratched at the door, snarling for release, and made the mother nervous.

Anger's smell filled the tomb in which the mother had buried her fear of it. It penetrated into the two small rooms, and the stench of the odor made the daughter ill.

The mother never recognized Anger's need to be let out. Instead she took the kitchen knife and tried to cut her wrist.

The mother never knew that Anger could be a friend, for Anger might have avoided her daughter's eagerness to leave home, in order to be on speaking terms with her own Anger, for one day the daughter came upon the story of Davida Angelica and for the first time in her life, she roared.

How many of us have been wounded by the arrow point of religion, bullied for years in the name of God? How many of us still carry the arrow point of a false faith that tries to manipulate God and when it doesn't work, disillusioned, never stop roaring?

Where is your repressed anger, your disappointment, your wound? New life is just underneath. Job's roarings poured out like water. Angel roared and her arrow point poured out. What wound is festering within you? What wound do you need to roar?

Reflect on the times you have felt angry, rejected, ugly, stupid, beaten, a failure. Write one of them out. Get in touch with any repressed anger you may have. The facts of the wound must be recognized before the act can be forgiven. Ask yourself, "What blocks me from healing and being whole? What can burn away a sense of failure? What can give me hope?"

Over and over Job cried out to God for justice. How many of us feel, seeing the misery and suffering of the world, "If only I were God..."

The Grimm Brothers told such a story, "The Goose Girl," which Joan Aiken has adapted[2]:

> One day God and Saint Peter were out walking, when Saint Peter burst out, "It must be a fine thing to be God! If I could only be God for even half a day, I would be content to be Saint Peter for ever after!"
>
> God smiled and granted Saint Peter's wish. "Be God until night fall!" God agreed.
>
> They went on together and soon saw a village ahead and a goose girl driving her flock of geese ahead of her. She shooed them into a meadow, then turned and left, walking back toward the village again.
>
> "Surely you won't leave your geese unguarded?" Saint Peter questioned.
>
> "It's a feast day!" she exclaimed. "You wouldn't expect me to stay?"
>
> "But who will look after the geese?" Saint Peter asked the goose girl.
>
> "God, of course!" she cried and ran off.
>
> "Well, Peter, you heard what she said!" God muffled a grin. "I am sorry you won't be going to the village feast, but since you are God until night fall, it's your job to protect them."

God walked toward the village and Saint Peter stayed behind to
mind the geese. Never again did he wish to be God!

Wisdom occurs when you have roared out your wounds so that they no longer bind you. Job roared, for Job was a person of integrity and courage, courage enough to protest to the Almighty for justice, for a trial in court, for an advocate. For Job had wealth and health and friends and family and the fear of the Lord one minute, and the next minute he was helpless.

Part 5

Two films have pictured for us how we can be in control one minute and helpless in the next. In *"Regarding Henry,"* Henry was changed overnight from a highly successful lawyer to a helpless vegetable of a person. In *"The Doctor,"* the cool, calculating, confident doctor, suddenly experienced what it meant to be a patient. The power of both films is that we see ourselves in their place. Whole today, helpless tomorrow. We cry, with Job, "Why me, Lord, what did I do to deserve this destruction?"

Through failure and our wounds we become vulnerable. Henry, the lawyer, became vulnerable. The doctor was vulnerable. Each of us is vulnerable. Each of us is in need of healing, "all have sinned," Paul reminds us. We pollute the air and sea and sky. We rail against nuclear power plants destroying the earth we love, as we sit in air conditioned homes and automobiles. We are trapped by the very system we have created and we fear the cost of the sacrifice. We curse and are cursed.

"The Doctor" learned compassion from a woman dying of cancer. After her death he received a letter from her in which she wrote the following story:

> There once was a farmer who set traps to catch animals and
> threw stones at them to keep them out of his fields. Then one day he
> became lonely and wanted them to return. He stood in the middle of
> the fields and stretched open his arms to them, but they were afraid
> of the new scarecrow.

She ended her letter and her story, "Only let down your arms, and we will come to you."

To feel vulnerable and afraid is to feel what others feel. Jesus was vulnerable and spread out his arms upon the cross, so that we may let down ours.

The world wounds us all, but some become healed in the Spirit. The world breaks everyone, but some become strong at the broken places. What shall separate us from the love of God? For me it is doubt, the fear to hope, that grips me with its teeth. I do not know whether Paul ever experienced doubt. I do not read it, but the "thorn in my flesh" is the demon Doubt. But if God is on our side, what have we to doubt or fear? Paul asks, "Who will accuse? Who will condemn? Who will separate?"

Will sorrow, or fear, or doubt, or poverty, or injustice? Will broken places, or broken hips, or broken relationships? Ill fortune is not God's rejection. God is not our enemy but our rescuer. God will not desert us! Surrounded by God's love, confident of God's grace, we can stone the demon Doubt to enthrone Trust and Hope in its place.

Paul writes his words with passion, for Paul's passion is God. He sings his conviction with joy, for that is faith—to give it a voice, for in the joy lies the wonder of the truth of the infinite love of God.

Paul's affirmation of faith, his piercing glimpse of victory, begins and ends with joy. "Nothing shall separate us from the love of God in Christ Jesus our Lord!"

If Paul had sat in an ivory tower, had not been beaten and bruised, jailed and persecuted, I could not believe his words, nor could I believe that God understands our sufferings and our needs, if Christ had not died a miserable death on the cross.

In <u>Preaching In Stories</u>[3] James A. Feehan tells the story of the end of time when billions of people were scattered on a great plain before God's throne. Most shrank back from the brillant light before them. But some groups near the front talked heatedly—not with cringing shame, but with belligerence.

> *"Can God judge us? How can he know about suffering?" snapped a pert young brunette. She ripped open a sleeve to reveal a tattooed number from a Nazi concentration camp. "We endured terror, beatings, torture, death!"*
>
> *In another group a Negro boy lowered his collar. "What about this?" he demanded, showing an ugly rope burn. "Lynched...for no crime but being black!"*
>
> *In another crowd, a pregnant school girl with sullen eyes murmured, "Why should I suffer. It wasn't my fault."*

Far out across the plain there were hundreds of such groups. Each had a complaint against God for the evil and suffering he permitted in his world. How lucky God was to live in heaven where all was sweetness and light, where there was no weeping or fear, no hunger or hatred. What did God know of all that man had been forced to endure in this world? For God leads a pretty sheltered life, they said.

So each of these groups sent forth their leader, chosen because he had suffered the most. A Jew, a Black, a person from Hiroshima, a horribly deformed arthritic, a thalidomide child. In the center of the plain they consulted with each other. At last they were ready to present their case. It was rather clever.

Before God could be qualified to be their judge, he must endure what they had endured. The decision was that God should be sentenced to live on earth—as a man!

Let him be born a Jew. Let the legitimacy of his birth be doubted. Give him work so difficult that even his family will think him out of his mind when he tries to do it. Let him be betrayed by his closest friends. Let him face false charges, be tried by a prejudiced jury and convicted by a cowardly judge. Let him be tortured. At the last, let him see what it means to be terribly alone. Then let him die. Let him die so that there can be no doubt that he died. Let there be a great host of witnesses to veryify it.

As each leader announced his portion of the sentence, loud murmurs of approval went up from the throng of people assembled.

And when the last had finished pronouncing sentence, there was a long silence. No one uttered another world. No one moved. For suddenly all knew that God had already served his sentence.

"What then are we to say about these things? If God is for us, who is against us?" "Who will separate us from the love of Christ?"

Paul knew sacrifice and pain; beatings and bruises and brokeness, persecution and imprisonment, and he knew even more the sacrifice and pain of his Christ. Paul interpreted his suffering through the cross and interpreted the cross through his suffering. Paul knew the wound of being human.

Remember his cry? "Wretched man that I am! Who will rescue me from this body of death?"

Paul heard the sound of the groanings of all of creation. And knowing all this, Paul interrupted with his affirmation of faith: "We know that all things work together for good for those who love God, who are called according to his purpose."

Just a minute, Paul. When you have lost your job, or your spouse, or the usefulness of your body, when you suffer and see suffering and injustice all about you, what does it mean that "all things work together for good for those who love God"? Does that mean that the poor and the dying, the abused and the suffering, do not love God enough? Is Paul promising too much? Perhaps before the wounds of the world and our own personal wounds the best thing would be to keep silent. Job didn't. Paul didn't, either. Paul interpreted his suffering through the cross of Christ.

We know..." Paul writes. How does Paul know that all things work together for good for those who love God? How do we know? For Paul cannot have our faith for us.

We know through faith based on tradition and scripture and reason and, as Paul,...experience. What are your experiences of God's grace? I recall the Christmas Eve my grown son asked his grandmother about the death of his grandfather, my father, who was killed when I was four years old, told in the story above. She told him how my father, being a car salesman, had delivered a new car to a customer and was returning with his old car, when he was catapulted into a passing train, not knowing the car had no brakes.

I knew that story, I had experienced that death, but this time she continued. "He wanted to take your mother with him, as he usually did, but she was only four years old and still taking naps, so he went alone."

All things are not good. My father's death was not good, but in everything God can work for good.

"We know that all things work together for good for those who love God, who are called according to God's purpose." What does it mean to be called? How are we called? Have you been called? How were you called? What does the voice of God sound like?

Or maybe we do not hear God's voice, God's calling, because our ears are blocked. God must dig out our ears. We have to lean into God's call, for the person beside you may hear nothing at all. Did those with Paul on the way to Damascus see the light that he saw? Did they hear the voice of Jesus that he heard? I wonder if Paul every wondered if he really heard, if he really saw? An inspiration, a voice heard, a figure seen, an experience, passes, but having experienced, heard, or seen, never passes.

The preacher Fred Craddock speaks of no longer speaking about his "call" to his family. He quit telling those Philistines! They would gather at his mother's house for a reunion and his brothers would ask, "Well, what shall we do? There's nothing to do. Let's have old Fred tell us about his call to the ministry." Dr. Craddock concludes, "I have never known God calling anyone loud enough for the whole family to hear. It was whispered."

Or maybe we do not hear God's voice because it is too risky. We fear and run from the call.

"We know that all things work together for good for those who love God, who are called according to God's purpose." For those whom God foreknew God also predestined, and those God predestined, God also called.

We are reminded in our study of the texts to be aware of the words that grab us, that disturb us. "Predestined" is a word that waves at me, so I am clued that there will be in my Bible study those who may see this word as a limitation of their freedom and unfairness on God's part. Those of you who believe in predestination are strengthened by that conviction. With Jeremiah you can say, "Before I formed you in the womb I knew you, and before you were born I consecrated you."

I think that all of us now and then, here and there, have experiences which make us wonder. I have told you of a four-year-old who was saved by a nap. You may substitute your own story of God's grace in your life.

What if we moved with and through suffering rather than against it? Happiness is not the goal of life, but living.

Keep or begin a journal. On the first page about halfway down draw a line from left to right and at the far left write the year you were born. At the far right pencil in the current year. Write six to eight significant events and dates in your personal spiritual history. Reflect on these as to how they reveal God's grace. If you are puzzled or disturbed by any of them, close your eyes and dialogue with it, as to what it wants to say to you or what God is trying to tell you. On the bottom of the time-line, write the "thread" that seems to weave them together. If you are in a group, share your insights with a partner or a small group, if you wish.

On the second page write the names of books or stories that have influenced your beliefs and behavior. Share with the group why these books have been influential. Then list the names of three persons who have made a significant impact on your life. Write a definition of healing prayer and one such experience you are willing to share with another.

What blocks you and me from experiencing God's love? What heaviness or fear or doubt? Share together your experience of suffering. What do Paul's words "All things work together for good for those who love God, who are called according to God's purpose" mean to you? Share in discussion.

Job questioned what he was experiencing for thirty-nine chapters in his cries for justice. Jesus' cry was briefer as he struggled to surrender to life's actions and to God. The Gethsemane prayer is one of doubt and we have all prayed it. "If you be willing, remove this cup, this suffering..."

"Nevertheless, Thy will be done."

What if the purpose of suffering is creative? What if the purpose of all of life, sickness and health, life and death, joy and sadness, is creative? What can we do to heal the pollution of body and mind, the sickness of doubt and despair, of meaninglessness and missionless-ness?

Suffering can be either a spur to thinking, speaking boldly (Is that why Paul was so bold in his preaching?), or that which separates one from society, God, and oneself.

A plot is the moving suspense of story from disequilibrium to resolution. Job protested out of the disequilibrium and disruptiveness of his suffering. Does suffering have any purpose? Can we order chaos and conflict?

The poet Dylan Thomas wrote a poem to his father who was dying, "Death Shall Have No Dominion," in which he told him to roar, to rage against the dying of the light.

The story of Job is the story of an honest man, a person of integrity and courage, the courage of Davida, courage enough to complain to God, to protest to the Almighty for justice, for a trial in court, for an advocate. How are our islands to meet? Where is our bridge to one another? To God?

Intellectual answers, abstract dogma and doctrine, are not enough. Job's friends' replies are devoid of feeling, of even having heard Job, and therefore, devoid of mercy.

I began the story of the wounded healer. I would end it as the retreat leader asked, "Are you willing to invite Jesus into your faith imagination?" after hearing the other's story.

"Take time with Jesus in your imagination. Talk with him. Give your anger to him."

The woman did not mean tomorrow, nor next week, nor sometime in the future. Her words meant now, and the wounded one wandered to the tiny prayer chapel the wise woman had built in her backyard. She sat in silence and waited. She waited for Jesus to come into her imagination, and it was a long wait.

"If you will not come back, as my father will not, then I will leave!" she spoke in her imagination, no longer the four-year-old, but an angry woman.

And Jesus replied, "Come sit on my lap."

The four-year-old refused.

Jesus smiled, and this time Jesus waited.

Slowly, cautiously, she came and crawled up into his lap.

"All children need daddies," he said, putting his arms around her. "I am sorry your daddy was killed. I cannot bring him back now, but I have a gift for you. Reach into my pocket."

Tenatively, shyly, she put her hand into the pocket of his robe and found...the gifts of imagination and trust.

She clasped them in her hand. She was no longer alone. She would never be alone again, for Jesus was with her. No one could take the gifts Jesus had given her. They were his virtues. She had not earned them. They were gifts, and in her imagination, suddenly her father was with her.

At last she knew that God the Parent was there and she was loved.

During Lent we feel the agony of the absence of God and cry out with Job, "Where is God?" and with Jesus, "Take this cup from me," until we remember, "There he is on the cross" and "Nevertheless Thy will be done." The one who stretched out his arms upon that symbol of human torture and cruelty, so that we might let down our arms to welcome God's embrace, transformed that symbol of our cruelty into the symbol of God, the Parent's love for us.

Part 6

Do a guided faith meditation: Sit comfortably, place your feet flat on the floor, hands in lap, eyes closed, and take a deep breath in ... and out..Imagine yourself in a small woods with sunlight coming between the leaves of the trees. You sit beside a small, flowing stream, and all is still around you. (Pause) Then Jesus comes and sits beside you. He puts his arm around your shoulder and you put your head on his shoulder and sit in the peace of the place together. Then Jesus asks you, "What is your heaviness, or fear, or doubt?" You speak to Jesus from the honesty of your heart. (Pause) You listen for Jesus' answer. (Pause) If not now, later. Then, knowing you can return to this place in your imagination whenever you like, return to this room and open your eyes.

Close with singing a hymn of thanksgiving and the following prayers:

Pray a Prayer of Confession: Forgive us and all mothers and fathers who have Anger as a constant companion, denying or locking it up in the cells of ourselves. Forgive those of us who never curb our tongues out of love, allowing those tongues to control us. Forgive those of us who are afraid to speak and confront conflict, who ignore or hide from its evil consequences.

Hear the Words of Assurance: Anger need neither be chained nor entertained, for I, the Lord your God, am your Healer and Redeemer. I am Love and you are loved. Amen.

Assignment: Read and meditate on Job 6:14-30.

[1]Beth A. Richardson, *Alive Now!* (Nashville: The Upper Room, May/June, 1991), p. 44.
[2]Joan Aiken, The Kingdom Under the Sea and Other Stories (New York: Penguin Books,1971).
[3]James A. Feehan, Preaching In Stories (Dublin: The Mercier Press, 1989), p.101.

"WHAT ARE FRIENDS FOR?"

Suggested format:
(10 minutes) Job story
(15 minutes) Story: "The Formula" and exercise
(10 minutes) Complete the sentence: Friends are for...
(10 minutes) Poem: "I Reach for Friendship" and exercise
(15 minutes) Simulation or story "The Beckoner"

Part 1

Job's cattle died, his sons and daughters died, his friends, all but three, left him, and his body was covered with sores. He sat in dust and ashes, in garbage, in misery, and his three friends sat with him in silence. On the third day they spoke.

Job wanted to know what he had done wrong. His friends told him, for what are friends for?

It is easy to criticize Job's friends. Before we learn what they say, let's pretend we are one of Job's friends. In one sentence what would you do or say to Job?

53

Job argued with them and protested to God. Job was not complaining as much about his suffering as he was that God was silent. God, who is the source of his hope, seemed not to hear.

Job's three friends provide the traditional answer of Israel, the covenantal relationship with Yahweh in which the good prosper and the evil suffer. But Israel is in exile and her experience does not fit the formula. What had she done to deserve this?

Job's friends gave Job, as many Western missionaries used to give the pagan natives, a theology divorced from their situation:"Here is tradition, now make your life fit it." They answered from a creed that had become a formula, the preservation of a doctrine, rather than from the pangs of creativity.

Added to the suffering God inflicted (or Satan, to whom God gave permission in the story), is now Job's disappointment in his friends whose religion blocked them from hearing or seeing. They intended only to "fix" Job's problem, to solve it for him with unexperienced doctrine.

Eliphaz, the first speaker, is intent upon developing the dogma of divine justice. He speaks brilliantly from the head, but there is no love conveyed, no compassion for Job's plight.

Dogma, doctrine, creeds are cold and, when unaccompanied by faith and love, are dead, "a shell deprived of its meat." Formulas, professional apologetics, may succeed with the mind but they fail the heart.

Eliphaz represents the objective scholar who presents only "the facts," or the official in the church who upholds only "the Law," neglecting the grace and gospel of God.

Part 2

Discuss: Have we abstracted God from the whole of life? How and where do you encounter God? What shapes your understanding of God? The hymns, the prayers, the sermons you hear and sing? How do you experience the presence of God? Is the province of God for you all of creation?

That God is God of the heart as well as the head hardly needs to be said. Yet how often we confine God to a single book, a specific time, and a particular place. God is beyond time and space, schedule and story, rules and requirements, doctrine and dogma.

> *The mystic was back from the desert. "Tell us," they said, "what God is like."*
>
> *But how could he ever tell them what he had experienced in his heart? Can God be put into words?*
>
> *He finally gave them a formula—so inaccurate, so inadequate— in the hope that some of them might be tempted to experience it for themselves.*
>
> *They seized upon the formula. They made it a sacred text. They imposed it on others as a holy belief. They went to great pains to spread it in foreign lands. Some even took the lives of others because of it.*
>
> *The mystic was sad. It might have been better if he had said nothing.*[1]

In one sentence write the "formula" by which you live and move and have your being.

Part 3

Job's friends have answers, formulas. Eliphaz tried to prove that "happy is the one the Lord reproves." "Thank you, Mr. Eliphaz, but no thank you. Punishment is not my cup of tea."

Bildad tried to defend divine justice, that God rewards the "good" and punishes the "bad." "Mr. Bildad, uncover your eyes and ears. Look and see."

Zophar told Job to repent. "Of being human, Mr. Zophar? Whose fault is that?"

Job's friends instructed Job out of their orthodox theology. Samuel Terrien wrote, "Theism as an intellectual formulation of a belief divorced from faith, loses contact with life. Ethical monotheism, when it provides a method for spelling out rationally the mystery of God, is utterly separated from the reality which it seeks to interpret. It negates God by the very fact that it claims to comprehend God. It creates an idol in the image of man's mind. The monotheism of the friends has become the mere projection of their idea of justice."[2]

Could it be that the friends are three aspects of Job himself, voices of his own conviction, belief, and doubt? He listens to the past and finds it comfortless. Eliphaz says not to aspire too high, be satisfied. Bildad and Zophar urge common sense, penitence and humility. None of Job's friends, however, touch him in his despair or come near the root of his problem. Job sees life as meaningless and cannot relate this to his idea of God.

Job's friends spoke out of their intellect while Job spoke out of his feelings and experiences. Job's friends wanted to fix it, for they had contacted a powerful case of meddling. Job, however, roared his protest out of his experience with God, his intimate relationship with God. God touched Job whole and Job spoke out of his body, his sores and his sufferings, becoming a parable for those who cry, "Show me!"

It is the destiny of each of us to be born, to live and struggle and to die, but Job the Hero, "blameless and upright" wanted to know why. Job was a faithful witness to the doubt and despair we encounter when we look at the world. Though he vascilated between ardent faith and desperate doubt, at the core of his being, the center of his doubt, there was faith.

What are friends for?" Most of us know the importance of relationships, for friendships that are creative, mutual and free. Complete the sentence "Friends are for..."

Humans have hungers, and one of the greatest hungers is the desire for significant relationships. We need to know we are of worth to others, for life is relational. As we are loved and accepted, we find personal growth and renewed energy. Loneliness is bearable if we do not feel abandoned and helpless.

Forget the formulas, Job is a lonely island.

"He has put my family far from me,
and my acquaintances are wholly estranged from me" (Job 19:13).

No one is an island," the poet wrote. No one is completely alone. "And therefore never send to know for whom the bell tolls; It tolls for thee."[3]

Nor is any "saying," such as the above, completely alone or completely true until the opposite is held in balance, for in another sense, each of us is an island. To be me is to be not-you.

"It tolls for thee," is a warning of suffering and death. In suffering we are united, one island, for suffering solidifies, helps us to empathize with the plight of others, but suffering also separates, making an individual island of each of us. Job cried, "I have become an alien in their eyes...my acquaintances are wholly estranged from me.." for Job's friends had never experienced what Job was suffering. They did not know, therefore, and their ignorance was a gulf between them. Job was, or at least Job felt, as an alien, an "island," in their eyes.

What do we do when we have not experienced and thus do not know? Sometimes we try to form that which is unknown into the known, the familiar. Job's friends told him what to do. Having never suffered Job's agony, it was all they had.

Have you ever felt as an alien, a stranger, a castaway on a desert island? When each of us is an island, we long for someone to connect us to mainland. Sometimes we look to our spouse or our child or our priest for that unconditional love only God can give.

When we long to be whole, to be one island, we grieve rather than praise our being.

"Margaret, are you grieving
Over Goldengrove unleaving?" the poet Gerard Manley Hopkins asked. Margaret was grieving because the tree was losing its leaves.
"Now, no matter, child, the name:
Sorrow's springs are the same.
Nor mouth had, no nor mind, expressed
What heart heard of, ghost guessed:
It is the blight man was born for,
It is Margaret you mourn for."[4]

Who is the Margaret you mourn for?

Carl Jung, healer of souls, worried that modern men and women had thrown out the soul, the sacred, and the story, for he saw the results and wrote that no patient of his over 35 had a problem which in the last resort was not that of finding a religious outlook on life. Not fixed formula nor dogma nor denomination, but the living Spirit within.

Margaret, Marvin, Beverly, Benjamin,
"Sorrow's springs are still the same...
It is the blight man was born for..."

Each of us bears the wound of being human, with smudges on our soul. How do we care for that which is not seen, nor touched, but only sensed? In the past the soul was in the care of the church. The world outside was uninterested. But when we awoke to the awareness that God was not bound by chains inside the church, that the chains were our making, we saw the world again as God's. We became partners with God in the care of the soul and its sacredness day by day.

God gives the growth while the church, through the telling of its sacred stories, plants the seed. But all trees "unleave," and for this Margaret grieves.

Most of us love the seasons. The growth and green of spring, the yellow warmth of summer, the orange and red and brown of fall, and the white of winter, but fall can bring grieving. The beauty of the riotious colors of the changing leaves ends in their leaving, and change, though necessary, causes sorrow, because we care. We weep with Margaret and we know why..."Sorrow's springs are still the same..It is the blight man was born for.."

Is it the leaves we mourn for?Or is it Margaret we are grieving?

What is the soul's grief? How do we define the unexplainable?

Early peoples took the soul seriously and told a story, for the soul prefers to sing and dance, imagine and tell stories, to accept the intuition and imagination, even the shortcomings of who we are.

Job grieved for Job and his friends told him what to do. We know no one can tell us wisely how to live our life. We search alone. We work alone. We are an island, be we Margaret or Job.

And yet, just as we can/cannot help Margaret and her grieving, we face within ourselves the beast who can become the beauty, when we love and care for our souls, and the very things that help us live our lives...fantasy, poetry, people, music, art, stories, religion, for we are created together. No one is an island.

Discuss: Who were Job's friends and what were their points of view? What did they want Job to do? Who were their authorities? With which friend do you agree? Make a list of your friends and behind each name write the characteristic you value in them.

This is the season of Lent and we who know the sacred story of the denial of Jesus by one of his friends and the betrayal by another, may wonder if Jesus ever asked, "What are friends for?"

This is my commandment," he said, "that you love one another as I have loved you. No one has greater love than this, to lay down one's life for one's friends" (John 15:12-13).

Part 4

I reach for friendship remembering
David and Jonathan, [5]
Ruth and Naomi, [6]
Jesus and his "beloved" disciple, [7]
The four friends and the paralytic, [8]
And Huck and Jim [9]
And Little Women [10]
Christopher Robin and Winnie-the-Pooh, [11]
Charlotte and Wilbur [12] and Toad and Rat [13]
And Jesse and Leslie [14]
And me and you.

I reach for friendship and compassion
And find betrayal and rejection,
For there is Job and his friends,
Whose ears are stuffed with words
Memorized,
Rotted,
Sanitary
Within a decaying sanctuary, or Sanforized and safe within...

I reach for friendship
And feel a hand
Scratched and mauled with angry nail prints
Of a fearful people,
Reaching out to me.

Read aloud the poem above and write a paraphrase of Psalm 23, using "The Lord is my Friend."

Love may seem simple from the outside, yet it is the most difficult of all tasks, that for which all work exists. Heaviness misses it. So does fear and doubt. It is a gift

God reverses our values and our perceptions. Through Christ's death, the pouring out of his life because of his love, the cross, the symbol of torture and humiliation, has been reversed.

The cross makes visceral sense. I cannot wrap my mind around the mystery of God but my instinct knows it is true. My faith imagination accepts that reality. When I turn to the

59

compassion and love of Christ, dying on a cross, that wounded one becomes my Savior.

I remember the story of a child who had the same blood type as his sister who was dying. When he was asked to give his blood, he was frightened, because he believed that he would be giving up his life for his sister. With tears in his eyes and fear in his heart, he agreed out of love for his sister. How much more Jesus loves us!

And so he beckons us to follow him in that love.

Part 5

Tell or read "The Beckoner."

> That's God there at the corner, two blocks ahead. The Beckoner. He whistles, and then with a sweeping gesture and a gleam in his eyes beckons me, "C'mon!" I go. I know from the other times he whistled that when I get to his 'corner" he'll be whistling a couple of blocks further on.
>
> Of course there are others and the adventure is a "together" one. We had discovered, in our bumbling way, that we could move along better together, though we still had to read the signs ourselves to know how to move on. It isn't always clear. The summons sometimes comes in the dusk or in the fog, and though we get general directions, in the long run, we do the major part of the mapping out. And there's a way in which our own mapping out influences the Beckoner.
>
> We find, as a matter of fact, that we are much better off when we opt to let the Beckoner play a large role in our lives—not in the sense of having life presented to us on the proverbial silver platter. The pioneer's life is more demanding than the settler's. To be a settler is to settle for less. But we get unnerved easily by the thought of not having genuine parking places, always the unknown.
>
> One of our people seems to have an inside track on the Beckoner—like he lives with him as well as with us. He can talk about him like he just came from table with him. (In a good family, table sharing is where you really find out about each other's lives and dreams.) Our Fellow is quite aware of his own special relationship with the Beckoner—in fact he calls him much more personal names than that. We have the strong sensation that to follow our Fellow is to be "right on"

with the Beckoner. It makes us feel a little more personal about the Beckoner, for we never did run fast enough to catch him at the next corner.

It is difficult to explain this Fellow. Some have said that he used to live with the Beckoner before he came among us. Other have said that he is truly Beckoner and truly Pioneer himself, without confusion. Still others have said that he is the Light, but that he shines with the Beckoner's own light; it's the Beckoner's true light, but it is also truly he (the Fellow) who does the shining. To be frank, he is a mystery to us. Yet a fact to us, as well.

We like picking his mind and being at table with him is about the best way any of us have found to pick his mind. Sometimes when he can't be there, we still do the table thing in his name; and he still works on our sensitivities, and if that isn't being "present," I don't know what is.

Life is still as fraught as ever with problems, but there is a certain confidence we have now as we move into the Future, knowing that only in movement-into-a-Future are we true to ourselves, true to the Fellow, and true to the Beckoner whom the Fellow says to call Father. And believe me, life stays a high adventure. [15]

Job's friends spoke out of their intellects. Job spoke out of his feelings. It is easier on the emotions to read or hear the speeches of Job's friends than to read or hear Job's. Job, speaking out of the deep feeling of dark pain, grabs our emotions and we identify with him in his predicament.

Job cried out of his experience with God, his intimate relationship with God, so intimate he could even lament, protest, complain. God touched Job whole. Job spoke out of his body, his sores and his sufferings, and thus became a parable for all persons, not only for "students" or pew-persons. Job was to be read as a clue, a model for those who cry, "Show me!" For what is he a parable for you, for suffering, integrity, arrogance, innocence? Or what?

It is not doctrines or dogmas that dry our tears. It is not creeds that comfort us in crises. It is in and through stories, stories such as the suffering of Job, that open us to the possibility and power of God's promises, God's love, and in our imagination the holding of God's hand and the writing of our names on its palm. Job as story connects chaos and order, integrates meaning, and transforms faith and worldview.

The book of Job is both confusing and satisfying to me. Given that the story evolves out of God allowing Satan to do what he likes with Job, it implies that God is in control. It is satisfying because the poets who wrote chapters 3-42 did not "write in" a God-answer for evil. We have been struggling with "Why evil?" ever since. It is the central problem for religious people.

Why a loving God permits suffering and injustice is difficult enough to handle, but to say that it is part of God's plan makes me, for one, cringe. My God is a loving God who hurts when I hurt.

To affirm this I must give up an omnipotent God or at least "understanding" with my rational mind. Reason is not a "light."

Four friends faced the grief.
Of one of them beyond belief.
"God gives, God takes away
Blessed be the Lord!" Job prayed.
Possessions gone, his children dead,
"Curse God and die," the mother said.
But Job replied, "No, God be praised!
I'll worship Him and take these evils, all of them;
Sores and suffering within, without,
My loving God I'll never doubt!
For if I take when God sends good,
I will accept this suffering, as I should.

Oh, evil words! Or words of trust
To help us face the future as we must?
"Job, Job," his three friends cried,
"Tell us the sin for which you're being tried?"
Their hollow words were mockery,
Sharp knives that jabbed him verbally.
"I am innocent!" was Job's cry,
Shaking the silence of the sky!
"If only God would hear my plea!
And see my pain, my agony.
Man, born of woman, is like a flower
That blooms and withers in an hour,
And when his breath is o'er,
Lies down in death and is no more.
Lord! let me live," Job cried,

"Let me love now
And if you will, Lord, show me how!

First Friend: "The wicked man, he writes in pain,
Only the righteous receive God's gain."
Praise be to God for every friend
And for their empty words that never end?
"But I am innocent! I do not fear.
I would face God if only he would hear.
I have not sinned, God, judge me,
I am innocent as any babe can be.
I have worshiped, obeyed, and trusted Thee.
But where are you, God?
Is God deaf, and blind, and dead,
Is there no God of mercy?"
Reading the Book of Job, I, this writer, said.

Second Friend: "The wicked suffer. God chastizes them.
The heavens, even the earth, refuses him
Whose heritage is decreed by God."
So spoke Job's second friend.
"This then," said Job, "is not the God I need,
Nor is the God that I will heed.
The wicked live, God smiles on them, they 'fly,'
While we together in desert lie?"

Third Friend: "Job, your light is darkened, you cannot see,
Repent, repent, live righteously."
"O," said Job, "curses on you, friend,
If only God would speak to me!
I have not turned from Him,
Why then does God turn from me?
Cannot God face my misery,
Unmoved Mover, look at me!"

Job's hurling "Why?" lies helplessly upon a neutral sky.
Silence...is Job's reply.
Then out of the Whirlwind God replied,
"Where were you when I created the heaven and earth?" God cried.
And Job was still.

1. Act out a simulation based upon the book of Job. Divide into groups of six to play: Job, Eliphaz, Bildad, Zophar, Elihu, God. Have Bibles for each participant. Job begins by lamenting (Job 3, 6-7, 12-14) and declaring his innocence. Eliphaz (4-5, 15, 22), Bildad (8, 18, 25), Zophar (11, 20), Elihu (33:19-37), God (38-41). Plan for an entire hour.

When the simulation is over rearrange the room and ask everyone to share their feelings, thoughts, and observations. Ask: What did you learn? What did you learn about the story of Job? Why do we feel we must defend or attack God for suffering, evil, and injustice?

Close with singing "What a Friend We Have In Jesus" and "Blest Be the Ties That Bind" and a prayer of thanksgiving for friendships.

Assignment: Read and meditation Chapter 7:1-6.

[1] Anthony de Mello, The Song of the Bird, Doubleday, Garden City, 1984.

[2] Samuel Terrien, The Elusive Presence (San Francisco: Harper & Row, 1978).

[3] John Donne, quoted by Frederick Buechner, The Hungering Dark (New York: Seabury, 1983).

[4] W. H, Gardner and N. H. MacKenzie, "Spring and Fall," The Poems of Gerard Manley Hopkins (New York: Oxford University Press, 1982).

[5] 1 Samuel 19 and 20.

[6] The book of "Ruth", Holy Bible.

[7] Some believe the beloved disciple is John.

[8] Mark 2:l-5.

[9] Mark Twain, Huckleberry Finn.

[10] Louisa Mae Alcott

[11] A.A Milne, Winnie-the-Pooh.

[12] E.B White, Charlotte's Web.

[13] Kenneth Grahme, The Wind in the Willow.

[14] Katherine Paterson, Bridge to Terabithia (New York: Harper Trophy, 1977).

[15] Bernard Lee, S.M., The Becoming of the Church (New York: Paulist Press, 1974) pp. 155-160.

MONTHS OF EMPTINESS AND NIGHTS OF MISERY

Suggested format:
(15 minutes) Story of the "Emille Bell"
(15 minutes) Relate to suffering and injustice
(10 minutes) Lecture on "An Awkward Thing"
(15 minutes) Discuss "Catcher in the Rye" and "Glittering Images"
(5 minutes) Guided faith meditation

Do not human beings have a
        hard service on earth,...
I am allotted months of empiness,
        and nights of misery are apportioned to me" (Job 7:1,3).

Part 1

Long, long ago there was an ancient bell that was famous for its beautiful tone. It had been commissioned by a king as a way of showing the people's devotion to Buddha. The king's advisors had told him that making a huge temple bell would secure the nation from foreign invasion. The specialist who cast the bell had produced several failures until he concluded that the only way to produce a great bell was to sacrifice a young maiden:

Soldiers were sent to find and fetch such a young girl. Coming upon a poor mother in a farm village with her small daughter, they took the child away, while she cried out piteously: "Emille, Emille!"— "Mother! O Mother!" When the molten lead and iron were prepared, the little girl was thrown into the fire. At last the bell maker succeeded. The bell, called the Emille Bell, made a sound more beautiful than any other.

When it rang, most people praised the art and the artist that had created such a beautiful sound. But whenever the mother whose child had been sacrificed heard it, her heart broke anew. Her neighbors, who knew of her sacrifice and pain, could not hear the beautiful tone without pain either.

Only those who understand the sacrifice can feel the pain. Others just enjoy the sound.[1]

The story of the suffering of Job is the story of the Emille bell. The poets of Job, seeing and feeling the suffering of those around them, allowed themselves the privilege of protest to Almighty God!

The suffering woman's friends understood her suffering and felt its pain as well. When the young die speechless, without the privilege of protest, we too cry with Job.

It is the destiny of each of us to be born, to live and struggle and to die, but Job, "blameless and upright" wanted to know why. Job is a witness to the doubt and despair all of us encounter when we look at the world in all its pain and suffering.

Discuss: What does it mean to be human (7:17) How does Job respond? Sit in silence and reflect on the story of "Emille Bell."

Why do we suffer? How do we live with suffering? What kind of God is it that is in charge of a world where the good suffer and the bad are rewarded? Is God good? How do we endure this existence? What can we do to heal the pollution of body and mind, the sickness of doubt and despair, of meaninglessness?

Choose one of the following questions and reflect on it: Have we abstracted God from the whole of life? How and where do you encounter God? What shapes your understanding of God? The hymns, the prayers, the sermons you hear and sing? How do you experience the presence of God? Who are we in relation to God? How do we explain or face the riddle of self and existence? Is there such a thing as disinterested piety? Is love its own reward? Can one give one's life for another? What is real? What is illusion? What is the palace of suffering? of feeling pain? of feeling anger? What is wisdom? Where is God? Write your own questions about suffering.

Bewildered, alone, in misery and doubt, Job represents all of us in our darkest hours of despair. Listen again to the text paraphrased: Before the mystery of God, I do not understand. I have no wisdom. This then is the gift I give, my lack of understanding, not to pretend to understand. Thomas said it, "Lord, I believe. Help my unbelief." Job and Thomas had faith at the core of their unfaith.

Job personified the riddle of suffering, showing that learning can come from pain and confusion. We are clay as Jeremiah and Isaiah suggest, and the Potter can do what the Potter wishes with the clay, but the clay, the work, can reveal to the artist what it is meant to be. The clay can "talk back." Abraham did (Genesis 18:27). Job did. Is suffering a way to grace, to constructive, creative potentiality?

Is it possible God will stop at nothing to transform our selfishness and suffering into a creative relationship of love? How can we use our sorrow? To live life forward is to create life out of what is given us, to make of it what is not yet, to discover the meaning of life in the miracle of creativity and imagination in a world filled with the sound of pain and suffering. Not only is there war and persecution and daily dying from hunger, there is in the last twenty years a doubling in the suicide rate. Boredom and the desire for intense excitement has led to an increased use of drugs and alcohol. For many a sense of hopelessness or meaninglessness, and a need for "instant gratification" are some of the reasons for suicide.

There are Emille bells in all our chapels and churches and homes. What do we do with their sound? Do we hide from it? Repress it? Deny it? Or bring it to God along with our trust and our pain? As we see the innocent suffer for the sins of the parents, we have a right to protest!

Part 2

Jooste Colin, a South African, tells the following story:

> I am a black, South African woman, 42, and have six children.
> We lived in a rural area, where my husband was a farmer with cattle.
> Then the government came and said we were harboring terrorists and
> were a security risk. They took us two hundred miles from home and
> dumped us in a camp. My husband had to work in the city and there
> he was found hanging from a tree. We are starving because there is
> no food and nowhere to find work.[2]

Evil has power. Child abuse is growing, the majority being cases of neglect. When babies birth babies, children are denied medical care, and poverty paves the streets of our cities, we listen to Isaiah's words of the lion and the calf lying down together. And to Woody Allen's, "The lion and the calf shall lie down together, but the calf won't get much sleep."[3]

It is dangerous to follow Jesus' teachings.
So we pray: ".. deliver us from evil:"
   In time of trial, deliver us from despair,
The bombs we make and store,
The land we pollute and cover with concrete.

The majority of humanity is suffering. Two-thirds of humanity experiences lack and injustice. "Forgive us our trespasses, our sin, as we forgive, for the failure to forgive is to place a tourniquet on God's mercy and love.

Have you ever experienced an injustice, unfairness, or suffering? What is the worst thing that has ever happened to you? Write it down. Feel it and study it. How did you feel at the time it happened? Give one descriptive word. How did you involve God in that event? What did you do? How do you feel about that event today? What questions are still unanswered? Write it all out and keep it private, if you will.

Job, an upright man, became a model of suffering, a brother to all sufferers and his story allowed the poets, using this ancient folktale, to ask their questions of the prevailing traditional theology of their time. Out of our confusion and pain when confronting evil, we cry to God, "Where are you? Why is heaven silent?" Our response is the cross looming up on our way through Lent.

To the secular world the cross makes no sense. It is foolishness. Even the Christian is sometimes confused by the doctrines that encrust the cross, choking out its message that this is where God is, involved in our daily, sinful, unfulfilled lives.

In order to allow us freedom to be truly human and holy, God persuades, shares power, and is with us in our tears. We see God in a vulnerable child born in a stable manger. We see Jesus, God's symbol of love, "despised and rejected," and if we stay with the sacred story long enough, we see God in a resurrected Christ, a stranger recognized in the breaking of bread, the symbol of his body given for a broken world.

Jesus wept over the sin and evil in the world, for he joined us in that world. And when we weep, Jesus weeps.

Job found no meaning in his suffering. "What's it all about?" he wanted to know. Suffering without meaning is cruel. For Job life was absurd. The reader, knowing God's wager with Satan, wonders if God took it too lightly. Was it God's apology to Job to enter that absurd humanity to become a suffering servant and through death to come to true life? What if we moved with and through suffering rather than against it?

When crabs discard their shells, they are extremely vulnerable until they create a new shell. How do you and I cope when our shells are cracked or removed? What happens when we fail or are hurt? How do we risk when our "mooring ropes" are removed? How do we "keep on" when all we seem to do is fail?

The alternative to suffering is meaning. We are not in charge of all of the circumstances in our lives, but we are in charge of how we will respond to them. I cannot determine how the ball will be pitched. I can decide how I will swing. I cannot determine the cards that will be dealt to me. I can decide how I will play them.

We can sit at a red light fuming and fussing or memorizing poetry and enjoying the present. To cultivate the art of living now as its own reward is to give meaning, is to cooperate with God in the work of creation and redemption. Dag Hammarskjold wrote in Markings: "On the day I first really believed in God, for the first time life made sense to me and the world had meaning."

I sometimes have a pain in my left shoulder blade. It used to make me angry. "Go away!" I would shout. Then I would meditate it "out." One day, however, when the sudden ache burst on me uninvited, I said without thinking, "What do you want, God?" I now use the pain as the way I see God tapping me on the shoulder to get my attention. I do not blame God for the pain. I only thank God for the awareness.

I wonder if God used Paul's "thorn of the flesh" to get his attention? I think it worked.

What do you do when you feel empty and it seems as if God is absent? There are times when all of us stumble in the dark. John Wesley reached a place in his life when he felt he could no longer preach. His spirit sagged, his faith was shriveling up. Before he gave up, however, he went to his spiritual director, Peter Bohler, who told him: "Preach faith until you have it, and then because you have it you will preach faith."

Max Beerbohm tells the story of a degenerate man who fell in love with an innocent woman. Because his face showed his past, he was distraught, until at last out of his need, he put on a mask to disguise his features, and she too fell in love with him. One day a woman from his past, out of malice, told him that she was going to reveal who he had been. Rather than having someone else tell his beloved, he decided he must do it himself. Pulling off the mask, he was shocked and surprised to discover that his face had taken on the features of the mask.

Yet one more story: A train raced down the track, unaware of the doom ahead. The telegraph wires were down and the track ahead had been destroyed by a flash flood. The station master grabbed his lighted lantern and ran through the downpouring rain. As he ran through the dark, stormy night he prayed he would reach the train in time, and then as he heard its whistle coming down the track, he tripped and his light went out. He shouted but his voice could not be heard above the storm's roar and the train's rumble, and not knowing what to do, he picked up the lantern and threw it into the cab's window where it hit the controls and brought the train to a stop.

Jesus said, "I have overcome the world." He did not say, "I have explained suffering in the world." And Paul added for him, "My grace is sufficient for you.." (2 Cor 12:9).

We cannot meet the challenge of suffering by reason alone, but trust helps us lift it into a higher level.

Jesus knew suffering. He knew his friends would suffer: "I send you forth as sheep in the midst of wolves."

Job questioned what he was experiencing for thirty-nine chapters in his cries for justice. Jesus' cry was briefer as he struggled to surrender to life's actions and to God. The Gethsemane prayer is one of doubt and we have all prayed it. "If you be willing, remove this cup, this suffering..."

Suffering is only redemptive when it is freely accepted. Jesus ended his prayer: "Nevertheless, Thy will be done." The entire prayer is the presentation of ourselves to God, the interchange of giving and receiving, which is the flow of love.

I asked creation to tell me about God
      and it blossomed.
I asked Jesus, the Christ,
      and he said, "This is my body, take the bread."

Part 3

It is just an awkward thing,
some boards, bent nails and string.
But I made it; it is mine
and more than mine, my dream's.
Dreams are delicate to share
they break with careless handling
and teased they fall apart.
No wonder children early learn
to hide their clumsy work
and husbands, silent in the night,
fail to share with their bored wives.
It is just an awkward thing.[4]

Sometimes we feel as if our life is just an awkward thing—but I made it. It is mine, and more than mine, my dream's.

What is life? To be more specific, what is my life, my dream's life? From what we can observe some persons choose money as their life's dream, others seem to choose success and fame. Still others prefer love or wisdom. What is your destiny, your destination, your dream and desire?

The poet says "dreams are delicate to share, they break with careless handling and teased they fall apart."

Do you remember the book or expression, "Why am I afraid to tell you who I am?" The answer to the question is, of course, because it is all we have and we do not want to be rejected. Rejection is an awkward thing.

I am a mature adult, a grandmother, and yet I still experience the fear of being vulnerable, of taking the risk of being rejected by the beloved. It is an awkward thing to be human, to feel the world's sorrow as our own, the pain that unites all humanity. When I hear of the suffering in black South Africa, I suffer. The wound of being human is an awkward thing.

It was an awkward thing, "some boards, bent nails," that cross on which Christ hung so long ago. Good Friday is an awkward thing and we do not dwell on death, for death is an awkward thing. Yet, with a sense of transcendence, that day was labeled "Good."

"Out of life comes death and out of death comes life," Heraclitus wrote, "out of the young the old, and out of the old the young, out of waking sleep and out of sleep waking, the stream of creation and dissolution never stops."

Dreams, whether conscious daydreams, desires, wishes, or unconscious fantasies are "delicate to share." They are delicate because we are afraid to be teased, to be misunderstood, to have our dreams broken with careless handling. As symbols of the unconscious even we ourselves do not understand their importance or meaning, although we intuit them. Our poverty of language limits our expression of them. Yet still we attempt to reflect and talk and write about such dreams, the unconscious and infinite. It is just an awkward thing.

Children early learn to hide their clumsy work, their failures, thier mistakes, for if you "really knew who I am, you might not love me as you do."

Where do children learn that love is only for the acceptable, the good, the successful? I know one way and it hurts me to say that at the most emotional time of the year, around the most emotional event of the year, Christmas, we tell children, "If you are not good Santa Claus will not come."

It hurts because first, it is a lie. "Santa Claus" wherever possible financially, spiritually, will come. Second, it is the birthday of the One through whom God revealed unconditional love for the unlovely, the not-good, the you and me of this world.

God said just the opposite: Because you are "not good," Jesus comes.

Once one of my sons was involved in a Cub Scout project that was judged for "best" and blue ribbons, and I saw the "products" that parents of small lads had made. Is winning more important than "clumsy work"? No wonder children early learn to hide their clumsy work, and in hiding their work, which is an expression of themselves, they learn to hide themselves.

We call it inferiority...our clumsy selves.

A positive self-image is the foundation of recovery, of health and healing. We stand outside many doors and choose which one we will open and enter.

George Bernard Shaw wrote, "People are always blaming their circumstances for being what they are. The people who get on in this world are the people who get up and look for the circumstances they want, and if they can't find them, make them."

All of us have tried "If only's." If only I had a better education, more patience, or money, better looks, more job opportunities, etc. When we let go of the "if only's" and claim the power to control the quality of our own lives, we can attempt to create our own destiny. Our choices shape our lives.

Self-esteem is the value we place upon ourselves. Self-image is the definition we have of ourselves. Jesus said, "Love your neighbor as yourself." How will you love your neighbor unless you know how to love yourself? You are special!

If you do not feel special, get to know yourself by asking yourself, "What are my potentials? What do I have to offer?" List the qualities that make you unique.

What you are is God's gift to you. What you make of yourself is your gift to God. A strong sense of personal identity is the product of independent thinking and an integrated set of values.

Defeat sets up defensiveness, defiance, which only increases the feeling of inferiority, and inferiority makes mutual recognition, and thus relationship, impossible, so "husbands, silent in the night, fail to share with bored wives." Inferiority is an awkward thing.

Husbands or wives who deliberately keep themselves unconscious or silent so as not to disturb a "satisfactory" marriage cannot know the joy of mutuality, that tender, brave, intimate, exasperating relationship.

Out of inferiority and fear we frequently look to another to complete ourselves. Husbands, wives, lovers feel alone, yet know they cannot make one another unalone. There is a solitude that no human companionship can take away, and when one expects the other to make them unalone, their feelings toward the other become a mixture of hope and disappointment. Psychological insecurity brings with it discord, separation, and "silence in the night." It is just an awkward thing.

"We are alone," however, is the paradox of "we are alone together in our aloneness." "Alone" is a combination of the words "all" and "one." To be alone can be to be "all one," whole: flesh and spirit, body and mind.

One's all-oneness is a sort of kinship with God wherebey we call the Unknown by a familiar name, although always meeting God in strange and unfamiliar guises.

Jesus used stories to describe the kingdom of heaven. The story of his cruxifiction, an awkward thing, ended in resurrection so that we can say and sing, through and with and because of every awkward thing, "I know that my Redeemer lives and I am loved with God's inestimable, unbelievable, love!"

I had read it once. Once was enough. Now ten years later I was asked to read it again for a class, God and Human Suffering. As I read Francois Mauriac's foreward to Elie Wisesel's <u>Night</u>, the sick stomach, the tense shoulder muscles, the tears, began, and I had not even started to read.

Two days before I had, with ninety others, spent a weekend with Frederick Buechner. I recalled now his remark that he never took a shower without thinking of the Holocaust.

Not to be vulnerable, sensitive, even sick, is to deny evil and so I read on: They celebrated Passover in the homes of the rabbis. This time the vicious angel of death did not pass over the homes of the Hebrews. This time God's elect, the Jews, were not escaping Pharaoh's hordes of soldiers. They were driven instead into the terrible arms and ovens of the Gestapo.

The hand that grasps upon hope is hard to pry open. To the very last moment, a germ of hope stayed alive in their hearts.

Draw a tree with branches on a large sheet of paper and attach it to the wall. Give each person a small piece of paper or cut out paper leaves and ask participants to write a sorrow or concern on it. Tape the leaves to the limbs and ask everyone to choose one leaf in a place of their own. Ask them to read their leaf aloud and what they would do about the grief and worry.

There is a Hasidic tale that tells how on the Day of Judgment each person will be allowed to hang his sorrows on the great Tree of Sorrows. When each person has hung his unhappiness on a limb, he may walk around the tree and choose a set of sufferings he prefers to his own. In the end each freely chooses to take back one's own rather than any of the others and leaves the Tree wiser than when he came.

Part 4

When I was a teenager I learned of 16-year-old Holden Caulfield. Knowing he is to be expelled from his fashionable prep school in PA, because of his poor grades, and because it is only a day or two before Christmas break, Holden decides to leave campus early and come home only when he was expected. The novel, <u>The Catcher in the Rye</u>, is Holden's story of those few days in New York City in relation to his past life.

Holden is a true romantic, at odds with the world because it is so distant from his dream of what the world should be. He sees phoniness all about him, but what is most disturbing is the lack of availability of people because of their inability to be honest, to run the risk of speaking the truth. Holden is looking for integrity.

In his search for love and truth, he listens but hears only noises. He seeks sincerity of presence of one person to another but finds only human solitude. It is only to his ten-year-old sister Phoebe he can speak his heart and hide nothing. Phoebe at last asks, "What do you really want to be, Holden?"

Holden replies, "I think I would like to be 'the catcher in the rye.'"

To break out of our loneliness, to reach out and touch another across the wall that separates, to catch one unaware before the mask returns, is to be a 'catcher in the rye.'

Being a teenager at the time, the story of Holden expressed my longing and loneliness. It was only later that I could return to Holden Caulfield and say, "You were blessed beyond reason, for you had one, at least one, to whom you could open your heart."

Discouraged by loneliness, even in a crowd, we seek insight into the meaning of human existence in the realm of personal experience. We seek one to whom we can open our heart, and out of that need we create for ourselves a personal spiritual space to discover the radical inwardness of the Spirit of God, the Source of life. We are not alone.

An old Hasidic story tells of the rabbi who asked his learned guests, "Where is the dwelling of God?"

Surprised at his question, they indicated, "All of creation is God's dwelling," and the rabbi, answering his own question, said, "The dwelling of God is wherever a person will let God in."

We are not alone. God is within and God is above and beyond.

The story of Job is the story of Holden, and the rest of us, seeking integrity and one to whom we can open our heart. Job was a man of integrity, who looked for honesty in his friends. Job was authentic to his experience. The poets of Job wrote their book out of their awareness and desire for their faith to be integral to their living day by day.

The gift of God is a model in which we see who we might be. In the awareness of who we are, we seek new birth "from above."

Holden and Job searched with integrity.

Fiction has a way of telling the truth, the truth that satisfies not just the intellect, the truth that cares for the soul. Susan Howatch has written a novel which she entitled, <u>Glittering Images</u>. the story of Charles Ashworth, a theological teacher in search for spiritual discernment.

Ashworth goes to a spiritual guide, Darrow, who sees that his need for "glittering images" has a stranglehold over him. Pleasing people is blackmailing him.

"When I know people like and approve of me," Ashworth said tentatively, "I don't feel so unfit and unworthy any more. If I don't feel unfit and unworthy, I won't be so dependent on people liking and approving of me and I won't need the glittering image to secure their liking and approval."

Ashworth went on to explain that he had two selves, the true self and the self who desired the glittering image.

Darrow asked, "How would your true self define success?"

Ashworth responded, "..Success is pursuing one's calling to the best of one's ability. In other words, one dedicates oneself to serving God, that is, one's true self, realizing the fullest potential for good of one's true self so that one's life is a harmonious expression of one's innate gifts."

Living a lie is to be out of harmony with one's true self, pursuing the wrong goals for the wrong reasons, caring more about other peoples' opinions than about serving God and doing God's will.

Darrow suggested that he needed to use his spiritual gifts to their full capacity, to spend time each day in training.

What are your spiritual gifts? What is the bread by which God feeds you at the banquet of life? How do you care for your soul? How do you "let God in"? Are you in harmony with your true self, using your spiritual gifts to their full capacity?

God offers God's creation as an answer, and wonder and worship is our response. Create in me a fresh heart, bless my eyes with wonder, let me see the star above and the little folk below who dance among us, so I may contemplate your wisdom and your work here on earth. God is beyond good and evil, even beyond experience. God shares human agony, transforming perplexity and agony of human existence into creation.

The sense of the holy, the sense of wonder, quickens one to action. Not the love of self but the love of life. So we pray with Paul: We are afflicted in every way, but not crushed. We are perplexed, but not driven to despair. We are persecuted, but not forsaken. Struck down, but not destroyed. Amen!

Part 5

Pray a guided faith imagery meditation: Let go of your heaviness now and sit quietly, your feet flat on the floor, eyes closed, hands in lap, back straight but body comfortable. Breathe in slowly to the count of three and breathe out to the same count three times.

The sun is shining. The day is warm. There is a slight breeze as you walk through the city. You observe the people. Some look happy. Some appear sad. Since you are in no hurry, you take time to smile at them, acknowledging their presence, seeing each of them as a child of God.

You find you have wandered to the city pool where the sick gather, for they believe that when the angel stirs the water, the first person to step into the pool will be cured, made well and whole.

You feel a sadness over their sickness and wish that you could help. You ask about their stories and learn that one man has been an invalid there for thirty-eight years and you subtract that from your age and think of how old you would have been when you became an invalid.

Someone is talking to the man now and you go closer to hear what he is saying. It is Jesus, the young rabbi and he is asking, "Do you want to be well?"

"Sir, I have no one to help me into the pool when the water is stirred. While I am trying to get in, someone else goes down ahead of me."

Jesus said to him, "Get up! Pick up your mat and walk."

At once the man was cured: he picked up his mat and walked.

When the man leaves you think about what you have just seen and heard and give thanks to God for Jesus and for health, for freedom of movement and wholeness.

Suddenly you are aware that symbloically you are stuck or paralyzed in some situation, or in some fear or problem. You think about what you would need to "let go" in order to be well or whole, to "pick up your mat and walk" for God.

Take time to talk with Jesus now.

Jesus smiles and hugs you and says kindly, "Accept my love that heals all wounds, for I love you as you are. I will take your hurt. That is the meaning of my cross. Now take my hand and get up. Pick up your mat and walk with me."

He holds your hand as you walk together. Imagine yourself cured, whole, happy, having accepted Jesus' hand, and what you will do now that you are healed.

When you are ready, knowing you can be with Jesus whenever you let go of your heaviness, return to this room.

Close with the singing of a hymn, such as, "There Is a Balm in Gilead," a prayer, and the benediction: Go now in trust that God the Creator of all that is hears our cries of protest and petition, that Christ is risen, and that the Holy Spirit shows to us the wonder of life through suffering and new birth. Amen.

Assignment: Read and meditate on Job 28.

[1] Editors John S. Pobee, Barbel von Wartenberg-Potter. New Eyes for Reading (Geneva: World Council of Churches, 1986) pp. 19-20.

[2] Colin, Jooset. Class on "South Africa," Lancaster Theological Seminary, January, 1980.

[3] Quoted by Mary Rose O'Rilley in "The Centered Classroom: Meditations on Teaching and Learning," in Weavings 4, No. 5 (Sept/Oct 1989) pp. 21-22.

[4] Jim Mayfield. Austin, Texas, from a book of private poems, 1971. Used by permission.

Session Five

"WHERE SHALL WISDOM
BE FOUND?"

Suggested format:
(15 minutes) Sharing Palm Sunday joy
(15 minutes) Lecture and list pieces of personal wisdom
(15 minutes) "Wisdom" and meditation
(15 minutes) Story: "Parabolic Story" and discuss "wise" persons

Part 1

It's Mardi Gras time! Cast off your heavy, conventional cloaks, the man from La Mancha has come, riding on an unbroken colt, the promise of God. It's a parade!

Look, the whole multitude is dancing in their undergarments. No masks here!

Listen, the whole multitude is praising God. No somber tones this day!

Only joy and celebration for all the deeds of power they had seen.

"Blessed is the king
Who comes in the name of the Lord!
Peace in heaven,
And glory in the highest!"
Alleluia! Alleluia!
Hip! Hip! Hurrah!
Jesus is coming!
Has come today!"

Can you see them? The people young and old, smiling, laughing, joyfully celebrating. This is their king! He has come! At last!

Can you hear them? "Alleluia! Behold our king comes!" What joy we celebrate on Palm Sunday!

It's hard to keep from singing and dancing with such good news!

When Mary heard the "good news" she sang her joy: "My spirit rejoices in God my Saviour.." and Mary's joy was contagious.

My four-year-old granddaughter's mother went on a two-week vacation with her three grown sisters and Lauren stayed with her daddy and me. Awakening in my bed, the day of her mother's return, Lauren, intutiting that all life is relational, smiled up at me and shouted, "My mommy's coming home, because it's tomorrow. There's always tomorrow!"

And when I call her long distance on the telephone I can hear her cry all the way to the telephone, "Grandma Elaine! Grandma Elaine!"

My granddaughter's cry brings me joy, for her joy is contagious.

THE LORD HAS NEED OF IT

This is a day for rejoicing.
This is the celebration of the king!
Let all the earth and heaven shout with joy.
"The Lord needs it."

For he said, "Go into the village and bring me
The colt that has never been ridden.
Just say this, "The Lord needs it."

A royal king?
One sent in the name of the Lord?
One who comes in deeds of power?
Almighty God,
Omniscent King,
Occupant of an unbroken colt?
The Lord needs it?

This is the one to whom we shout
"Hosanna! Save us!"?
But if God has needs, then we are involved.
Discipleship can be difficult.

"Why are you untying the colt?" its owners asked.
They said, "The Lord needs it."
"That is all," they said?
Discipleship can make fools of us all.
For they threw their cloaks on the colt for Jesus to sit on.

"Where are you?" God cried in the garden.
"I hid because I was naked and afraid."

And as he rode along, people kept spreading
Their cloaks on the way.
No need for masks nor sacred coverings this day.
This is the day for dancing.
This is the celebration of my Lord?

"Blessed is the king who comes in the name of the Lord!
Peace in heaven and glory in the highest!"

"And suddenly there was a multitude of the heavenly host
Praising God and saying,
'Glory to God in the hightest heaven,..'"

The stones of the earth
And the angels of the heaven
Praised God joyfully with a loud voice
And a multitude of disciples.

For this is a day for rejoicing!
This is the celebration of our Lord and King!
The Lord has need of it.

We celebrate our Lord and King!

The story, however, goes on... "And some of the Pharisees in the multitude said to him, 'Teacher, order your disciples to stop.' "

Is there always someone to rain on our parade? Is this a carnival or a processional to death? For the Pharisees this was serious business. No time for revelry now. They were concerned.

We have all experienced joy dampened, flooded with a seriousness of life and death in a violent world. How did Jesus answer?

"I tell you, if these were silent, the stones would shout out."

They did not know who Jesus was! This was a cosmic Lord, king of all creation!

"Rejoice! Rejoice always!" Paul sang. Where there is joy, give it a voice, for to miss the joy is to miss all. In the joy is the meaning of the action.

The glory of God is a person fully alive. This is the wisdom of God, the awe and celebration of the Lord.

Create a joy journal and list the activities that you enjoy doing. Divide your list into five sections:
    a. joys that can be claimed in 2-5 minutes
    b. 5-30 minutes
    c. 30 minutes to half a day
    d. half a day or longer
    e. dreams

Observe over the next few days on what brings you joy and record your observations.

Spend time with "high fantasy" of your own choosing. Write it out in your joy journal. It can renew your joy when you are "down" and return to it.

In pairs share some joy or gift you have received since the last time we met together.

(five minutes each) Say aloud a one-sentence prayer incorporating that joy.

Part 2

With time they learned that Jesus was not the kind of king they expected and he became "Wisdom."

Job asked, "Where then does wisdom come from?
And where is the place of understanding?..."
"Truly, the fear of the Lord, that is wisdom;
            and to depart from evil is understanding" (Job 28:20-28).

Along with the joy there are times of frustration when we just do not "get it." It makes no sense to the head or the heart. From where then does wisdom come?

During an ecumenical meeting of ministers Jesus entered the room and said, "A new commandment I give you." The Methodist said, "Is it moral?"
The Lutheran asked, "Is it Lutheran?"
The Presbyterian inquired, "Is it intellectual?"
The Pentecostal querried, "Is it ecstatic?"
The Episcopalian questioned, "Is it traditional?"
The Baptist asked, "Is it biblical?"
And Jesus replied, as he left the room, "Forget it, friends!"

In Mark's gospel even Jesus' disciples did not "get it." Where shall wisdom be found?

For the Hebrew, wisdom is not knowledge but obedience to the Torah, the teaching of and for the community. For Job's friends it is right orthodoxy. For the wisdom tradition it is not "right answers," but seeing something new, asking ultimate questions, and pondering the inaccessibility of wisdom, for wisdom belongs to God alone. Job said, "It is hidden from the eyes of all living,.." (28:21)

An ancient Hindu story says that the god of wisdom, believing that wisdom was not good for humanity, and jealous of his wisdom and his power, asked himself where he could hide it. Deciding that humans could climb to the tallest mountain and sink to the depths of the sea, he looked here and there for a place where he could hide wisdom. At last he decided to put it where humans would never think to look. He placed wisdom within their hearts.

83

Palm Sunday is a turning point in the life of Jesus. Chapter 28 is a turning point in the book of Job. It is a turning point in the life of Job, as well. Job declared that wisdom belongs to God. You and I do not possess wisdom, but we might be given wisdom as a gift, as manna in the wilderness. On the other hand wisdom is not a "thing" to be had, but something one lives into. You can dip into wisdom. You cannot damn it up. Wisdom is as water in your hands. Open your hands and it is gone.

Which of the following defines wisdom:
1. the right answer?
2. seeing with new eyes?
3. God's voice?
4. your experience?
5. what tradition (the church) has written?
6. the skill of living life in the presence of God?

Discuss the responses.

Part 3

Where is wisdom found? I suspect that I (and Job) are perhaps asking the wrong question of God. I really want to ask, "Where then does, not wisdom, but mercy come from?" I need a God who collects the tears of God's children, who hears their questions and their cries, and responds by being there.

Tears are a way of praying. Our tears of pleasure are prayers of praise and our tears of pain are pleas of petition. When Job suffered the anguish of his loss of family, wealth, and well-being, his friends sat with him for seven days, meaning "a long time!" They sat in silence, and I think, they sat with tears.

Job cried (3:24) "My only food is sighs, and my groans pour out like water."

God is the One who collects our tears, feels our pain, suffers our sorrow.

God cares and in wisdom may "hold back."

A man in India, wishing great wealth, prayed to the goddess of wealth, Kakshmi, begging her to make him rich.
He prayed to her for ten years to no avail, no effect, after which period of time he no

longer desired wealth but true happiness.

One day as he was meditating he say before him a beautiful woman, shining as if she were gold.

"Who are you? What are you doing here?"

"I am the goddess Lakshmi. I have heard your prayer and am here to grant your desire."

"Too late, my dear goddess. I have found the bliss of prayer and lost my desire for money. But tell me, why did you wait so long in coming?"

"To tell you the truth," she replied, "given the nature of the rites you so faithfully performed, you had fully earned the wealth. But in my love for you and your well being, and in my wisdom, I held back."

The Wisdom tradition of which the book of Job is a part, personifies wisdom, whose name in Greek is Sophia. She is the embodiment of compassion, creativity, nurturing, and relationship.

Yet, for Job, wisdom cannot be found. "The deep says, 'It is not in me,' and the sea says, 'It is not with me'" (Job 28:14).

In late Judaism there was a widespread belief in Sophia as Revealer of Wisdom, as well as defining Wisdom in terms of Law and Torah.

Baruch (3:20-30) asked concerning Wisdom: "Who has gone up into heaven and taken her, and brought her down from the clouds? Who has gone over the sea and found her, and will bury her for pure gold?" And again (4:1): "She is the book of the commandments of God, and the law that endures forever." God's gracious election of Israel and his gift of the Torah (Wisdom) brought God's word "near you."

Wisdom literature builds bridges between our traditions and our experiences. Wisdom literatrue shows me that it is appropriate to ask questions and to use our imagination to discuss and express the gap between the tradition's and the individual's experience. It is across that gap that poetic insight bridges and in that tension that great art is produced.

Jesus, as Lord of all creation and "wisdom," said that if we were silent, the stones would cry out. God is about to cry out of the whirlwind. Poetry, as God's answer to Job in the whirlwind, is not a logical disposal of the problem, but the distillation of a mood in the light of which the poet is able to carry on.

Two of the most important factors in learning wisdom are openness to experience and nature and a basic trust, which is the meaning of faith. God's wisdom is paradoxical; a both/and connection, a relationship. In the union of seeming opposites creation is renewed;

85

bliss and pain, gain and loss, Palm Sunday and Resurrection.

All things in time are pairs of opposites, yet there is a level of consciousness that transcends all catagories or forms, that transcends all pairs and integrates them in wholeness and harmony in All. That which transcends all names, notions, or "masks" for the Unknown, is expressed in silence in meditation, in sound in story and music, in action in touch and movement, and in the senses in worship and service.

Center yourself by closing your eyes, placing your feet on the floor and hands in your lap, sitting erect but comfortably, and breathing deeply. When you feel quiet within, ask for the gift of the Holy Spirit. Spend five minutes in silent contemplation, thinking about the gifts God has given you. As images and thoughts and feelings come and go, write them down. Think about their meaning to you now. Fantasize doing what you would most like to do and name the talents essential for that fantasy to become real. List the risks you would have to take. List what you would have to give up. List the obstacles you foresee.

The book of Job is the story of doubt whose core was trust, absolute faith, because Job waited, even with impatience, upon the good pleasure of God. It is the tension of Job's need to approach God as equal vs his integrity. Is defiance a sign of the hero-ine's virtue or crime, the assurance of God's love or egotism? Job expected to meet God on Job's terms, to obtain vindication of his rights. Job insisted that life was more paradoxical than his friends allowed.

Part 4

The wisdom tradition affirmed the "appropriateness" and orderliness of creation. Lyle Watson, reknown scholar, spoke to the Isthmus Institute Conference in Dallas, Texas on April 2l, l989 concerning "appropriateness" in nature, substantiating his thesis that there is a predisposition to appropriateness in animal, human, and earth.

He told of a missionary who cleared a field for the cannibals to play soccer and though there were fierce struggles for the ball, every game in the last seven years had ended in a draw. The young priest was confused. Then frustrated. "Don't you know that the object of the game is to beat the other team?" he shouted with great agitation.

The two captains smiled, calmly explaining to the priest, "No, Father, that is not the way of things. If someone wins, someone would have to lose."

Wisdom is the awareness of balance, of timeliness, of all things having their "season."

"Appropriateness" is a characteristic of Israel's wisdom tradition, "the right saying for the right occasion."

> They asked the rabbi how he always knew the right story for the right ocassion and he replied, "I will explain my parabolic method by telling you a story: There was once a merchant's son who wished to become a fine marksman and he went to school and won many awards and graduated with great honor. As he was returning home, his horses became thirsty and he stopped in a barn for them to drink. As he looked around the barn, he was amazed. The bull's eye had been hit in every single target. He asked the people of the village who their great marksman was and they were puzzled. "The only person who plays in that barn is a young Jewish lad." "Bring him to me," he said. When the boy entered the barn, he saw a small boy in a torn shirt and with barefeet. "How did you learn to aim so well?" he asked. Now the boy was puzzled. "Look," said the merchant's son, "you have hit the bull's eye every time. The boy began to smile and the marksman pointed to the targets. "I take my arrow and bow and shoot. Then I take a piece of chalk and draw a circle around where it lands." The rabbi finished his story, saying, "And by storing the stories in my mind, that is how I find the right story for the right ocassion." (An old Hasidic story)

Most of us, trained by a technological society (even within the church) are uncomfortable with "You are right" and "You are right." We ask, "But how can they both be right?" To which the wise teacher replies, "And you are right!"

We want to know in order to control. But the Hebrew word for knowing means to love.

> When the Civil War was over, Abraham Lincoln, the president, said, "Now we must heal the wounds of the nation. Now we must love and take care of all of the people."
>
> One of the Congressmen, still bitter and angry, stood up and pounded on the table, shouting, "Mr. Lincoln! I think our enemies ought to be destroyed!"
>
> Mr. Lincoln looked at the Congressman and slowly and softly said, "Mr. Stevens, do not I destroy my enemy when I make him my friend?"

Christianity is a religion of love and starting all over again. The Christian faith affirms that we are loved by God and in that grace we are liberated and energized. Grace happens to us when we encounter others in the spirit of love. We are called to be candles in a darkened room.

I like the new (old) designation of Passion Sunday for Palm Sunday. What does "Palm Sunday" really tell us except that people waved tree branches. But "passion" says a heap more.

There are few things today that people are "passionate" about. I admire those who are passionate about the earth, who place their bodies at her disposal, when the police haul the land "protectors" off to jail. Our laws and our officials seem to be taking Mother Earth for granted, nay worse, abusing and destroying her who has cared for them all of their lives. And I abhor "passion" in the hands of a few technocrats who elevate power above people, politicians who protect the wealthy from the health hazards of nuclear industry but ignore the poor and powerless.

I admire those who are passionate against the violence in the home, the nation, and the world. Passion Sunday begins the week of Jesus' passion that ended on the cross. A theology of love and a passion for justice have never been popular.

Raymond Brown, the New Testament scholar writes:
> *"We readers or hearers are meant to participate by asking ourselves how we would have stood in relation to the trial and crucifixion of Jesus. With which character in the narrative would I identify myself? The distribution of palms in church may too quickly assure me that I would have been among the crowd that hailed Jesus appreciatively. Is it not more likely that I might have been among the disciples who fled from danger, abandoning him? Or at moments in my life have I not played the role of Peter, denying, or even Judas betraying him? Have I not found myself like Johannine Pilate, trying to avoid a decision between good and evil? Or like the Matthean Pilate have I made a bad decision and then washed my hands so that the record could show that I was blameless? Or most likely of all, might I not have stood among the religious leaders who condemned Jesus?"*[1]

Choose to do one from the following:

- List three "wise" people who have had the most influence on your life, their positive qualities, and how they relate to you. Include contemporaries and people you know personally. Then brainstorm with the entire group.

- Form a circle and ask each participant to say what they like about each of the others in the circle. If the group is large, form several circles.

- Think of the times you have been lonely , or if you are lonely now, make a list of alternative activities you might do. Share lists with the entire group. On a scale of I to I0, I being worst and I0 the best, what number would you give to solitude? to loneliness? Discuss the five things "not to do" when talking with someone who is lonely and change them into positive statements.

- Choose a partner and take turns discussing one problem you are facing. Brainstorm possible solutions.

- In silence and openness reflect on God's will for your life now. Pray for the wisdom to see yourself as the precious, unique individual that you are, with special interests and gifts, thoughts and feelings.

- Or, pray for the wisdom to see your future as the work of your own hands and heart and the courage to take responsibility for choosing your own direction.

So we pray for discernment, for wisdom. Sometimes we discern and sometimes we do not, for God's thoughts are not our thoughts. It reminds me of Michael Lindvall's story of the Motorcycle and Carmen:

> The Motorcycle and Carmen had given her mother "fits" all the time she was growing up. Now, in the hospital from a motorcycle accident in which her boyfriend was killed, Carmen had a vision. During her long hospital stay she learned to paint for therapy and painted her vision—a long haried, white-robed Jesus on a motorcycle, not wearing a helmet! She gave it to the minister to hang in the entrance of the church for people to see it as they entered. However, his wife put it on the boiler room door, and when Carmen's mother saw that, she did something about it. The next time the minister entered the sanctuary, he saw the picture hanging for all to see as they entered. Lifting the picture from the wall, he read the note underneath: "Do Not Remove This Picture. God Meant It To Be Here!"[2]

Lindvall concluded his story of Carmen saying that it is hard to believe people change much, but sometimes they do. Grace does not necessarily move along the paths we know, the ways that are comfortable for us. Who knows what image the Divine may choose? We never could manipulate God into catering to our wants, no more than the ancient Jacob could make a deal with God. Yet even Jesus in the garden asked for the cup to be removed. He knew well enough, however, to add, "Thy will be done," for Jesus was the Wisdom of God.

"Blessed is the king who comes in the name of the Lord!"

Palm Sunday is a symbolic act that expresses our yearning for a sight of God, or a sound, a glimpse, or smell, a whisp of God's perfume, a transformation from being stuck in the material to dancing with the Spirit.

It expresses our need for celebrating; thanking and praising God for deeds of grace and power, the mighty acts of God, for singing, for we are singers of life and not death.

Paul cried out, "Who will 'save' me?" I cry, "Who will help me to an awareness of God in the ordinary everyday, release me from the demons of doubt and fear?"

Jesus is our metaphor for union with God, for sensing his sonship and living out of that knowledge and trust.

Some people act as if they understand God so well they have lost the fear and mystery of God. Others doubt the existence of God because of God's seeming absence and silence in the face of cosmic evil and injustice.

The book of Job takes contemporary form in the television evangelists who usurp God's holiness and Third World citizens who are innocent before a seemingly inactive God.

The story says that God is God and there are no other gods and that God's ways are not our ways.

The season of Lent is the season of sacred stories. Telling stories during Lent gives substance to our hopes and fears, our loves and hates, our faith and doubt, the good and evil in our lives. They are our inner selves speaking the language of the imagination.

Lent is a time for remembering the stories of Jesus' happy entrance into Jerusalem on Palm Sunday, of his Last Supper with his friends, of his trials before Annas and Pilate, the horror of crucifixion, and the golry of his resurrection.

Jesus announced his mission as that of preaching good news to the poor, proclaiming release to the captives, recovering of sight to the blind, setting at liberty those who are oppressed and, and proclaiming the acceptable year of the Lord (Luke 4:18-19). And when he died on the cross, he claimed, "It is accomplished!"

As his followers in the church we are partially healed, we are partly whole, but we cannot cry with Christ, "It is accomplished!" for God is not finished with us yet.

When Jesus stood up to read from Isaiah, it was not only to "proclaim' but to fulfill the words of the prophet. He was that Word and when he said, "It is finished!" it was accomplished!

When I was a child and would hear those words each Lenten season, I thought of Jesus' work as a burden. After all, dying on a cross is not very appealing to a child. Jesus's words then meant to me, "At last it is over. I have finally done it and can go 'home' to peace and love and leave this evil world."

Therefore, it was exciting when I recently heard the words. "It is accomplished!" and Jesus' death meant, "Whee! I did it! Triumph and victory all for your glory, Abba!"

Read Romans 11:33 as a prayer of affirmation. Close with the reading of the poem and the singing of a hymn:

> The fear of the Lord is upon us.
> The time for remembering has come.
> The mountains shout God's majesty.
> Earth shows forth God's honor.
> The merciful flowers bloom
> And the seas and heavens endure forever.
> The faithful grain begins to sing,
> And all God's wonderful works join in the chorus,
> "Blessed is the king of the Lord!
> Peace in heaven and glory in the highest!"
> With the stones and angels we sing God's praise!
> This is the beginning of wisdom.
> This is understanding.

Stand up and say "Yes!" to life, to love, and to your own power to make positive decisions.

Assignment: Read and reflect on Job 38:1-42:17.

[1] James A. Feehan, <u>Preaching in Stories</u> (Dublin: The Mercier Press, 1989) p. 104.
[2] Michael Lindvall, <u>Good News from North Haven</u> (New York: Doubleday, 1991).

UTTERING VS. UNDERSTANDING

Suggested format:
(5 minutes) Discuss Job and John 20
(15 minutes) Read and discuss resurrection stories
(15minutes) Discuss Lazarus story and death
(10 minutes) Write affirmations of faith
(15 minutes) Summary and closure
Or (22 minutes): View *The Parable* (color, sound, 16 mm film or video. Order from Mass Media Ministries, 800-828-8825. Ages 12 & up). It is the story of a clown who ministers to others in a traveling circus symbolizes the Passion of Jesus with his struggles and self-sacrifice. It has received world-wide recognition.

"I had heard of you by the hearing of the ear,
             but now my eye sees you;" (Job 42:5).

Part 1

After 37 chapters of "talk;" advice, laments, complaints, God finally answered Job out of the whirlwind. God paraded his creation before Job, with a sense of astonishment and joy at what God had done! "Explanation is not the only attitude by which to approach the world, Job!"

"Explanation," having facts without compassion and wonder, is not the only attitude by which to approach the world. Is wisdom not understandable without explanation, or love without understanding?

Explanation kills wonder. Try seeing a sunset in the company of one who explains the phenomenon, or the act of love. There are times for words and times for wonder, and the time for wonder is not always the time for words. Jesus said, "don't babble." Well, not in so many words. He might just as well have put his finger on his lips and said, "Shhh!"

We ask, from our perspective, "Is God just the way we are just?" "Shhhh!" Look! Listen! Learn from nature and the poets the grandeur of God. Viewing creation, you cannot help but hope.

God did not answer Job's question concerning justice. Out of the whirlwind God pointed to God's creation and said, in not so many words: "Celebrate love and creation! Dare to love and create in a world that does not know the love that set the stars in motion and created out of holy imagination."

God asked Job, "Where were you when I created the world. Am I not more than and free from any picture or image you have of me, Job? Look at the wonder of my creation! Remember, Job, you are the creature. I am the Creator."

Creation affirms the Creator. The wisdom tradition is a way of seeing and being in the world, affirming the blessings of God in creation and suggesting that nature itself is a manifestation of God. The spirit of the divine is the breath within us. Thus, we recognize ourselves as one with nature and take Incarnation seriously. The universe is the Thought of God, the Action of Christ, and the Power of the Spirit. Israel through its wisdom literature recognized the unity between Creator and creation.

Creation is a gift. Grace is not grace if it depends on human achievement, but to benefit by it one must, as a coat, put it on. In our "newness," our conversion or renewal we share the coat. We share with others our seeing and our joy of living.

To explain Mystery with words, to substitute rote, memorized doctrine and creed for experiencing, worshiping God, to moan and groan before the Almighty, is cause for frustration. Job just didn't understand the grand design of the cosmos, any more than we understand the mystery of Easter resurrection!

At last Job said, "I had heard of you by the hearing of the ear, but now my eye sees you;"

Perhaps we make sense out of the mysteries of life by being thrown into the mire. Not by thinking and talking about it but learning it in the nitty-gritty, daily struggle to make a life.

Then God said to Job, "Shall a faultfinder contend with the Almighty? Anyone who argues with God must respond" (40:2).

Job replied that he did not have an answer...at last! "I have uttered what I did not understand, things too wonderful for me, which I did not know" (40:3).

The Wisdom tradition is interested in forming character, not adding knowledge. There is more than having facts. What is the significance of these facts, and to explain is to kill wonder.

God encourages us to look at God's Creation and on Easter Sunday, God's Incarnation and Resurrection.

Read John 20:1-18.

"When she (Mary) had said this, she turned around and saw Jesus standing there.." (John 20:14).

In John's Revelation of Jesus Christ, he tells of his vision on the island of Patmos, and the words he heard, and he wrote, "I turned around to see the voice that was speaking to me."

Hearing, seeing, is the way we live day by day in an ordinary world. Hearing and seeing are two of the five senses we take for granted, and yet they are crucial to our faith. The heard and seen Scripture engages the whole person, body and spirit, mind and senses through the imagination, for the sensory imagination is sacramental.

When Job questioned God, God did not give a reply to his question, but suggested that Job "look around." Job wanted a way of seeing God's presence built into the universe, the revelation of God that is constantly present, yet always filtered through the framework

of our present perception. What God wanted for Job was a sense of wonder.

Before Job "saw" God, he did not see wonder. I wonder how God would answer Job today? Have we lost the ability to look and to see with wonder as well? Are we no longer sensitive to the mystery and beauty of nature? Do we not long for a return to a sense of wonder, of contemplating God's work with praise and thanksgiving? Where have we lost the joy or participation in the creativity of God?

Job wanted a human answer, a reasonable, rational argument for the proof of the righteousness of God, and God answered Job out of the whirlwind, listing God's achievements in creation. Was Job asking the wrong question, seeking the inappropriate answer from the divine-human relationship?

God astonished Job, overwhelmed him, for with rhapsody and a sense of wonder God seemed astonished at what God had done! God saw that it was good! So God did not "explain" to Job, God showed.

Seeing is about intimacy, relationship. Job lived his relationship with God out of a formula. Now the "formula" had become "rotted words." It did not match his experience.

Job had knowlege about God, but he did not know God.

Part 2

Charles Laughton, the famous actor, read the 23rd Psalm with his magnificent voice and skill. Once he listened to an old, uneducated woman recite the psalm by heart and tears filled his eyes. Afterward a friend, having noticed, asked what had happened. Laughton replied, "I know the psalm. She knows the Shepherd."

Knowledge has to do with skills or accumulations of information. Wisdom has to do with intimacy.

In the Christian tradition Jesus' parables were intended to show how God is present in everyday life.

When God spoke out of the whirlwind, Job answered, "I had heard of you by the hearing of the ear, but now my eye sees you;" (Job 42:5).

Did Job mean that he saw God in a physical form? Or is seeing a way of "perceiving," a seeing that fills our whole being to become an attitude, a way of living in the world? For Job (and the Christian) I believe such seeing is faith, and I ask who is educating us into this kind of seeing today? For what meaning you get out of the text depends on which picture you take into the text. I wonder what Job would have thought if he had looked at nature with all the marvels we have today?

It takes time and awareness to look into our loved one's eyes, or at a tree or a sunset, a bird or a flower, but when you do, you just might see God. What if we "heard" God if we listened with our eyes?

"Blessed are the eyes that see what you see, kings and prophets longed to see that, but did not..." (Lk 10:23-24).

Job gained his insight into God through pain and suffering and has become a metaphor, a parable, for us today. We live with Job in our anguish, crying, "Where are you, the loving, righteous God we have been taught, the One who rewards the good and punishes the evil?"How do we live now that our lives are disrupted? How do we hope and cope with tragedy? What does one do with experience that does not fit the community's teaching? What is the place of experience? of tradition? of scripture? of reason?

Job gained his "knowledge," his wisdom through his experience. God took Job's "old" seeing and transformed it into "new" seeing, a relationship of intimacy.

"Let the people see," said the Master of the Universe. We tell God's story so that we may help others see with new eyes and hear with new ears and in Christ become new beings.

> A rabbi once boasted to another rabbi that evenings he saw the angel who rolls away the light before the darkness, and mornings the angel who rolls away the darkness before the light. The other replied, "Yes, in my youth I saw that too. Later on you don't see these things any more." It's all a matter of seeing.

Reflect on what things you no longer "see." Ponder why.

> At a camp ground a young minister was the speaker. He had three children and one morning his wife said to them, "Today you must play right here in our backyard and not go roaming off."
> They were disappointed but knew better than to complain. The

ten-year-old boy leaped up from his seat at the breakast table and shouted, "Let's play ball. First batter!" Immediately his eight-year-old brother called out, "Second batter!" That left the small six-year-old sister with the short straw. Their father wondered if she would say, "I got gypped. It is not fair and I am not going to play!" Or would she whine drearily, "O.K. I will play but I won't like it!" Instead, she did neither of these but quickly and enthusiastically leaped from her chair, shouting, "Third batter!"

It is not what happens, but how we view what happens. Sometimes the only thing we can change is our attitude.

One person sees only the problem and acts accordingly. The other sees an opportunity and it makes all the difference.

Self-esteem is based on our perception of our worth.

To be content, to see life as our wish-come-true, affects who we are.

To be aware of the "life within" is to be aware of "unseen things." God is the Center around which new patterns of events constellate in time. When one experiences a sense of God's love through a perspective that permeates and provides inner power and external purpose, one experiences a sense of well-being and confidence. To be content, to see life as our wish-come-true affects who we are.

How did Mary and John see? Mary turned around to see Jesus. John turned around to see what he had heard. Job looked around. "Turning around" implies conversion, transformation, action seeing in a new way, with a new perception. I think we call it "faith." Suddenly something extraordinary enters our world and we turn around, and when we do, we become awake and aware of Jesus' living presence in our lives.

Both Mary and John heard and saw the living Word for themselves.

God in creativity implied that Job was asking the wrong question. He was trying to pen God into a jox of justice, refusing God freedom to be God.

God's response to evil in showing Job creation is the language of contemplation and worship, for its message is not social or theological isolation but hints of the intelligent and mysterious power that moves creation and deserves our worship.

Job had heard of God, the traditional belief by hearsy inherited from the past, but now Job "saw" God. He moved from the intellect to the joy of communion and love, after which one can then confess and surrender the ego. And Satan sourily sulked away.

There is another gift God graciously gives us. It is the gift of imagination. Having at times identified with Job and his story, I too have been angry at God and complained, but there are times when my imagination says to me, "God will stop at nothing to save you from your self-centered desires, which cause you to seek your own good above your neighbor's. God will stop at nothing to redeem and restore the relationship you have broken."

Job's final response to God and all that had happened to him was to "repent in dust and ashes." Job confessed because he trusted God.

Grace is not grace if it depends on human achievement, but to benefit by it one must, as a coat, put it on. In our "newness," our conversion or renewal we will share the coat.

Samuel Terrien wrote of Job that having now felt the gift of grace, the spring of self-knowledge without despair, he can borrow the wildness to rejoice. Accepting the gift of conversion leads to creative vocation.

For what does God reward Job? For changing his mind or for his steadfast defiance, standing on his own two feet, refusing to lie before the Creator of the univese? Does Job surrender in reconciliation or submit in passive resignation? does Job repent in failure or rejoice in success? Of what does Job repent or rejoice? Does he repent or change his mind about how he sees things? Were Job's expectations false expectations of God? The Joban poets do not "let us off the hook," as the saying goes. From the beginning of the poem to the end, it is "what you see is what you get."

Wisdom literature emphsizes the eye as opposed to Israel's "ear," the hearing of God's word: "Thou shalt make no images of God!"

In "A Masque of Reason" Robert Frost has God thanking Job for freeing him by giving the gift of choice, allowing God to play the game by his own rules. Read and discuss the following:

> "I've had you on my mind a thousand years
> To thank you someday for the way you helped me
> Establish once for all the principle
> There's no connection man can reason out
> Between his just deserts and what he gets.

Virtue may fail and wickedness succeed.
'Twas a great demonstration we put on.
I should have spoken sooner had I found
The word I wanted. You would have supposed
One who in the beginning was the Word
Would be in a position to command it.
It had to seem unmeaning to have meaning,
And it came out all right. I have no doubt
You realize by now the part you played
To stultify the Deuteronomist
And change the tenor of religious thought.
My thanks are to you for releasing me
From moral bondage to the human race.
The only free will there at first was man's,
Who could do good or evil as he chose.
I had no choice but I must follow him
With forfeits and rewards he understood—
Unless I liked to suffer loss of worship.
I had to prosper good and punish evil.
You changed all that. You set me free to reign."[1]

These stories by which we are fed and around which this community has gathered, are breathed alive with each telling. So we ask the story, "What difference does it make if Jesus was alive to John and Mary and Thomas and is not alive to us today?"

If we do not accept his love, or hear him call us by our name, or let us touch him with our spirit, then our faith is in vain, as Paul wrote, "If Christ has not been raised, then our preaching is in vain and your faith is in vain." (I Corinthians I5:I4)

But Jesus came to them and stood among them and said, "Peace be with you." And Jesus is here in our midst this morning, the living Jesus, the resurrected Jesus, having come to us in love, saying to us, "Martha, Mary, calling us by our name, "Touch my hand, and remember that your name is written on the palm of my hand. You may not have seen me with your physical eyes, but through prayer and story see me now with your spiritual eyes, and hear this sacred story:

Because Jesus lives, was raised from the dead, we are new beings. Because the earth, whose skies and seas and lands we have polluted, whose foundations are shaking, who waits with eager longing, groaning in travail, especially on this the Earth's Day, therefore, we will...

The story is unended for the story goes on. Each of us writes an ending by the way we live and believe, for we are God's stories, and through prayer and the sacred story we can love, hear our name called, touch Jesus and believe, for these stories were written so that you and I may believe that Jesus is the Christ, the Son of God, and by believeing have life in his name.

Guided Meditation Prayer: Invite persons to close their eyes and center. Read slowly:
Peter and the beloved disciple run to the tomb and you follow them. When the beloved disciple reaches the tomb, he looks inside. "The grave cloths are still there," he says.

Peter enters the tomb and sees the grave cloths in one place and the face cloth in another, and the beloved disciple enters, looks and believes.

Then Peter and the beloved disciple return home. Now you are alone. Jesus is dead. His body is gone. You stand outside the tomb and cry. When you finally look inside, you see two angels dressed in white, one sitting at the head and the other at the feet where the body of Jesus had been. They ask, "Why are you crying?"

"They took my Lord and I do not know where they put him."

A new voice speaks. "Why are you crying? For whom are you looking?"

It must be the gardner. "If you have taken him away, tell me where you have put him."

He calls you by name! Listen to Jesus call you by your name now. Turn and speak to him, telling him what is on your heart.

As you approach him, he says, "Do not touch me, but go and tell my friends that I am going to my Father and your Father, my God and your God."

You sit in the silence alone, in amazement, too shocked to move. Jesus is alive! Jesus is not dead! You jump up and run to tell the others, "I have seen the Lord! This is what he said!"

When you are ready, return to this place, knowing you can be with Jesus whenever you want, and open your eyes.

We began with Ash Wednesday, sitting with Job and his three friends in silence on the garbage heap. We close with the story of Jesus hanging silently on a cross between two thieves on the town's garbage heap. That is where he died and that is why.

Nauseous we turn from its putrid smell, its toxic stink, until we remember the odor in the stable was probably just as offensive.

This is the incarnation of our Deity? What incredible love!

The living God is God in unlimited freedom and we miss God when we try to limit God by our ideas and expectations.

Job encountered God in his misery, his suffering. He then compared his "hearing" of God to being with God, experiencing God, which he called "seeing".

The poets want us to experience the living God rather than a lifeless doctrine about God, a word-concept of God. Job is dumbfounded conceptually. How can it be? But living with God, the reality of God's presence in freedom, Job's brokenness is overwhelmed, replaced.

"It is a lot different having cancer than talking about it."

Part 3

Lazarus, the brother of Mary and Martha, was ill in Bethany. So the sisters sent a message to Jesus, "Lord, he whom you love is ill." But when Jesus heard, he said, "This illness does not lead to death. It is for God's glory," and he stayed two days longer where he was.

Then he said to his disciples, "Let us go to Judea again," and his disciples reminded him how some of the Jews had tried to stone him. "Why would you go again?"

Jesus explained that Lazarus had fallen asleep and when they did not understand, he said, "Lazarus is dead. For your sake I am glad I was not there, so that you may believe.

When he arrived, Jesus found Lazarus had been dead for four days and Martha went out to meet him. "Lord, if you had been here, my brother would not have died."

"Your brother will rise again," Jesus told her.

"I know that he will rise again in the resurrection on the last day."

Jesus said to her, "I am the resurrection and the life. Do you believe this?"

"Yes, Lord, I believe that you are the Messiah, the Son of God."

Then Jesus went to the tomb and prayed to God, calling to Lararus, "Come out!" and Jesus said to them, "Unbind him, and let him go."

Many of Jesus' followers believed in him. But some of them planned to put him to death.

"Lord," Martha said to Jesus, "if you had been here, my brother would not have died."

"If only you had been here!" In the March 13, 1985 issue of "The Christian Century" Frederick H. Borsch tells of the harrowing, griping story of being aboard a DC 10 that shot off the end of the runway into Boston Harbor. His account in "Where Was God When the

Plane Crashed?" is chilling, and frightening, and his reflections are revealing and thought-provoking. He raises the perennial problem "Is God there? How much does God do?"

Borsch writes of Theology A and Theology B. A says, "If my children survive, if my doctor gives me a good report, if my business thrives, then I will give thanks and trust God." B says, "Even though I walk through the valley of death, I fear no evil, for you are with me."

Borsch reports, "The God who cannot be seen is yet present as the Spirit of all that is, willing to share in the consequences of creation—including evil and suffering—and seeking to transform them through love."

"When Jesus saw Mary weeping, and the Jews who had come along with her also weeping, he was deeply moved in spirit and troubled...Jesus wept." God does not run away in the presence of death.

Yet even in despair we do not welcome death.

Death is giving up the old so the new may be born, but death, a painful separation from loved ones, causes tears. When Jesus had cried, he prayed, and then he said, "Lazarus, come out!" And Lazarus did.

"Take off the grave clothes and let him go."

For those who have suffered the death of a loved one, there comes the time to hear, "Let go the mourning, the grief, the hanging on to that which is dead. Rejoice, for God's glory."

After the resurrection we can say, "for God's glory."

Jesus knew resurrection now was hard to believe, for he had said to his disciples, Lazarus' death is so that you might believe. He said to Martha, "I am the resurrection. Do you believe this?" He said to God, "Father, I thank you for having heard me. I knew that you always hear me, but I have said this for the sake of the crowd standing here, so that they may believe that you sent me."

In small groups or pairs talk about your feelings about death. Have you ever lost something or someone very meaningful to you? What was most helpful to you in your grief? What frightens you most about death? What causes you the most grief? What are your questions about death?

Imagine death in a physical form and describe it or give it a metaphor. List the euphonisms for death and dying and what they say to you . Dialogue with Death. Name some of the stories or films you can recall concerning death. Relate them to the Resurrection story and write an epitaph for Jesus' tombstone.

Resurrection now, unbinding you and me today, is hard to believe. How are you and I bound? Where is our unbinding? Walter Wangerin, Jr., as a father wrote a letter to his daughter:[2]

"I snapped at you last week. I could justify my anger, I suppose, with good reasons, historically accurate reasons..but then I would miss your hug, and my forgiveness, and the face of Jesus in my daughter's face."

The action took place in San Francisco, near the end of a California choir tour, on the way home to Indiana, the father being responsible for the lot of them, for over a hundred pieces of baggage, two lost tickets, tension through thick traffic, and then just minutes before boarding, the actor Danny Glover signing autographs for Mary. The father swam through people to retrieve his daughter, gone however before he got there, and instead, lying on the floor as trash, was Mary's airplane ticket!

When Mary emerged from the public restroom, her father snapped at her and she put down her head and cried. He had wiped out Holy Week for her, for pettiness can be so deadly.

Only forgiveness is the regeneration of all the good that was and all that ought to be, and on the plane he knelt beside her seat and told her his sin and sorrow. He whispered his confession rather than his reasons, and she turned and hugged him, and the week became holy again, for this was the meaning of the passion. In that hug was resurrection.

We are daily bound and then suddenly there is resurrection, whether from an emergency in which we saw our death and from which we emerged and survived, or a transformation of an idea, feeling, or experience, from doubt and depression to hope and healing, an experience of rebirth, the transformation of the fear of death to the trust of resurrection..all because of our "believings."

Resurrection now? So thought the Nobel physicist Erwin Schrodinger: "For eternally and always there is only now, one and the same now; the present is the only thing that has no end."[3] What do you believe?

As Jesus is present in the sacrament of the Eucharist, Jesus is present in our resurrection from the dead, for Jesus came to raise the dead. In the beginning the Word brought creation out of nothing. In the end the Word will bring a new heaven and a new earth out of nothing but death.

A strange story...resurrection...for some a "fairy tale," a "happy-ever-after" story, that lifts our hearts and feeds our spirits, giving us a fleeting glimpse of the joy "beyond the walls of the world,"a high and glorious story for the glory of God. Resurrection now? We still must work, and suffer, and hope and die, but now that we believe, we are alive in Christ. This was the purpose of John's sacred story.."These stories were written so that you may believe that Jesus is the Christ, the Son of God, and that by believing, you may have life in his name."

Lord, I believe. Help me in my unbelief. Unbind me so I may live in Christ, resurrected for today. Amen.

This is the day we celebrate the empty cross and the empty tomb. Christ is risen! He is risen indeed!

Part 4

Read and reflect on the resurrection theme in Job 19:25-27, Job's repentance: 40:3-5 and 42:1-6. Why does Job repent? What does it mean? Of what does he repent, and on Job's words in 42:1-6. What do they mean to you?

Discuss: Do we make sense out of the mysteries of life by being thrown into the mire? Who is responsible, God or me?

Write an affirmation of faith including death and beyond, such as: I believe that new life is possible through the power of a loving God.

Part 5

Conclude this study by discussing what has been presented in this class. Summarize your thoughts. Close by standing and reading aloud your affirmations of faith or sing a

life-affirming song and close with a prayer.

[1] Collected Poems of Robert Frost.
[2] Walter Wangerin, Jr., The Manger Is Empty (San Francisco: Harper & Row, 1989).
[3] Erwin Schrodinger, My View of the World (Woodbridge, CT: DH Bow, 1983), p. 22.